A Day

with

Dori

Compilation of Daily Posts of

Living Your Best Life

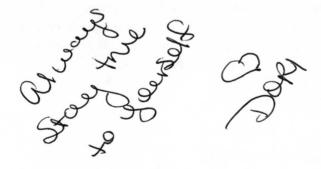

Always
Stay true
to yourself
♡ Dori

DORI MARTEN

ISBN 978-1-63874-427-6 (paperback)
ISBN 978-1-63874-428-3 (digital)

Christian Faith Publishing, Inc.
832 Park Avenue
Meadville, PA 16335
www.christianfaithpublishing.com

Printed in the United States of America

I'm just me. I get up every day and get done what needs doing. I saddle my own horses, drive my own trucks, and take care of what's mine. I didn't "get lucky" in life. I've gotten where I am out of pure survival. I could have been another statistic. I decided not to be. I was a teenage mother with no college education, four kids by twenty-four years old, divorced at the age of thirty-two. I didn't blame society. I didn't stop doing what was necessary because life didn't go as planned.

My kids were my responsibility. They didn't get to choose their life, so I owed it to them to provide the best I could at the time and improve our lives along the way. I took chances, I made mistakes. Life knocked me down, and I got back up. I kept pushing forward even when it seemed like it wasn't getting me anywhere. I took a chance buying my first dump truck. I took another chance with my brokerage business. I knew my life needed to change, so I changed it. I didn't wait for anyone to do it for me. I did it for myself. If you want to change, change. It might be scary, you might screw up. So what? Then change again.

#adaywithdori
#grit
#determination

Contents

Windshield Time and Random Thoughts

Things I've learned so far today:

1. There's a fine line between confidence and arrogance.
2. Jealousy is ugly. Don't be ugly.
3. Morals are a rare quality. Embrace them.
4. Being kind is free. Sprinkle that shit everywhere.
5. If you're cheating in life, you are the only one getting cheated.
6. Honesty is actually a good quality. Try it.

#adaywithdori
#toomuchwindshieldtime
#randomthoughts

Treat others the way you want to be treated.
Be humble and kind.
Say something nice.
Smile at a stranger.
Wave at your neighbors.
Beauty shines in your actions, not your reflection in a mirror.

#adaywithdori
#haveagoodheart

As I sit here on hold on this job site, I'm thinking of the conversations I've had with people this week. Some have been uplifting and life changing. Others have been the kind that makes you wonder just what is wrong with society.

It is sad to me that people pretend to be things they aren't, place blame on places it doesn't belong to make themselves look better. There is something to learn everyday of life. No one knows it all. While I've been through my share of ups and downs, someone else always has things a little bit worse. Be nice, be kind, be respectful, be human, and if you can't do those things, be quiet!

It is only failure if you allow it to be.

You can allow it to weigh you down or use those things that don't work out right the first time as stepping stones to success.

#adaywithdori
#besuccessful

It's okay

- To want to have kids
- To not want kids
- To get married
- To stay single
- To be a stay-at-home parent
- To be a working parent
- To have a girls' weekend
- To stay home on the couch
- To rent an apartment
- To buy a house
- To sleep in
- To wake up early
- To have a staycation
- To travel aboard
- To play sports
- To read books
- To go to college
- To barely have a high school diploma

It's all okay.
As long as at the end of the day, it's what's best for you and yours.

It is not okay

- To judge others
- To expect someone to take care of you
- To speak poorly of your own child's other family
- To be mean
- To be abusive
- To be a bully or manipulative

Seriously. Just be a good person.
Before you point fingers and judge others, make sure you are perfect
and always have been.

Never take criticism from someone you wouldn't go to for advice.

#adaywithdori
#beagoodperson
#dowhatsbestforyou
#itsokay

Life can be a series of sunshine and storms. Enjoy the sunny days and stay strong through the storms. Remember even if it rains for days, it won't rain forever.

#adaywithdori
#strongerthenthestorm
#randomthoughts

Highlights of a conversation I had today:

- Live alone for a significant amount of time at least once in your life. Pay for everything yourself. No help from your parents, grandparents, boyfriend, etc. Live on mac and cheese with a mattress in the floor.
- You'll outgrow people. And it's okay.
- It's just a job, 100 percent not worth being treated poorly over.
- Not having a reaction is still a reaction. Some situations need to be addressed.
- What you allow in your life will be what continues.
- If a cycle needs to be broken, break it.
- Your childhood isn't an excuse. You're an adult now. Face your fears.
- If you have kids, parent them whether you're a young parent, old parent or in between. That child didn't ask to be born, so step up and do your job.
- Always have a Plan B income. You can't predict the future.
- You teach people how to treat you by what you allow.
- If you hit a rough patch in life, reach out for help.
- You are changeable.
- You are worthy.
- You are important.

#adaywithdori
#liveyourbestlife

I was asked today to share some sort of inspiration (via Facebook) to a graduating senior after finding out that high school is done forever

I've struggled all afternoon in my head with this task

There are so many important things you know you'll be missing out on, and it is 100 percent okay to be frustrated with all of life right now.

What isn't okay is to stop living.
It isn't okay to dwell on all you'll miss out on.

It is, however, okay and more than likely necessary to grieve for it all

- for what would have been your last day of school
- for senior skip day
- for prom (hopefully, somehow, this will still happen)
- for sports
- and band concerts

And the rest of everything that goes with your senior year.

Once you've grieved,
Move on.
Move on to your whole future.
 (I'm sure right now, you could care less about the future.)
But learning to move through tough situations is part of life.
It's unfortunate.
It's complicated.
However, at the end of the day, it is reality.

Now is the time to take the down time. As absolutely boring and mind numbing as it is, down time is necessary, and learning to be bored is honestly a good thing.

Your graduating class will be remembered forever for the creative ways you spend the remainder of these days. These will be lifelong memories

Make these memories and cherish them.
Just because you don't get to do the "traditional" senior year things
Doesn't mean you and your friends won't still make lifetime memories.

Life gave me a different path my senior year
I didn't attend prom or walk the stage
I left school in January of my senior year and never once had regrets.
Granted mine was a personal choice and not taken from me.
I'm just sharing about my path strictly because one day you'll realize it was all okay to not get to do the traditional "stuff."
Life will one day be bigger than a few months of your senior year.
Until you get to that point mentally, grieve for your loss.
Then pick it all up and show this big ole world what you're made of.

#adaywithdori
#senioryear2020

Today's thoughts:

1. Don't mistake a hand up for a hand out.
2. Don't mistake kindness for ignorance.
3. Respect is earned, not given freely.
4. Don't be jealous of what someone else has. Work harder for yourself.
5. Treat others the way you want to be treated.

#adaywithdori

Weight
We automatically think of the scale, the mirror, or our britches size.

However,
Sometimes the extra weight we carry in our mind, heart, and soul is
what we truly need to shed

Feed your body with good foods.
Feed your mind, heart, and soul with good things too.
Good thoughts
Positive self-talk
Walk away from toxicity and drama.
Do not allow anyone to steal your joy.

Take some "me" time and restore your good energy.
It is not selfish, it is completely necessary.

#adaywithdori
#notallweightisonthebody
#begoodtoyou
#mindheartsoul

I notice.
I notice things others don't.
I notice subtle suggestions.
I notice those odd looks.
I notice the bad body language.
I notice the lone person in a crowd.
I notice the attention seeker.
I notice the shady guy.

I notice these things because life hasn't always been easy or fair.
I notice because I don't trust many.

I notice because I've been done wrong.
I notice because I've been the girl they talk about when I leave the table.

I notice because some of the roads I've walked down, I refuse to walk again.

#adaywithdori
#inotice

Two of the hardest tests in life: the patience to wait for the right moment and the courage to accept that you have waited for nothing.

So many people are afraid.

Afraid to

- fail
- succeed
- move away
- change jobs
- go to college
- date
- break up
- start a family
- walk away from negativity

If you never try,
You'll never know
If your circle is not shouting,
"Go for it,"
You need a new circle.

If you were meant to stay in one place and only be one thing,
God would not have given us feet.
He would have given us roots.

#adaywithdori
#dontliveafraid
#leavethesmallmindsinthedust
#takethechance

Random thoughts:

- Don't expect more out of others than you do from yourself.
- Give respect to get respect.
- Treat others the way you want to be treated.
- Never treat someone else's child better than you treat your own.
- Work hard.
- Never mix business and pleasure.
- Be professional at work no matter your career choice.
- Loyalty is rare. Cherish those that are loyal to you.
- What others are doing isn't your business.
- This is the only body you have. Treat it well.
- Have hobbies.
- Your kids and job are not hobbies.
- You are your only competition.
- Enjoy solitude.
- Treasure true friends.
- Understand true friends do not need to talk daily, weekly, or even monthly.
- A walk in nature is a great antidepressant.
- A home is to be lived in, not to be looked at.
- Be to others who you needed when you were young.
- Life is all about balance.
- How pretty you look will never be as important as how pretty you are.
- If they gossip with you, they'll gossip about you.
- Never trust a liar no matter how small the lie.
- Yesterday's mistakes won't change tomorrow's successes.
- No matter how strong you are, we all get to have bad days.
- It's okay to cry.
- Everything is better after a good nap.
- Do what makes your soul happy.

#adaywithdori
#randomthoughts
#windshieldtime

These people I admire the most:

- Are the ones that will stand up for what's right, not for what's easy
- Will put a stop to a bully either for themselves or others
- Do the right thing, even when no one is watching
- Will treat everyone with respect whether they mow your yard or are your doctor
- Takes time for those that look up to them
- Aren't afraid to tell their story of struggles, knowing it could change someone's life
- Get up and work hard every day, never expecting a hand-out, although always willing to give a hand up
- Are never jealous of what others have. They know the grass is greenest where it's watered most.
- Take care of their family without complaints or excuses, oftentimes taking that dreaded job because it will pay the bills
- Will talk to someone before ever talking about them

#adaywithdori
#beadmirable
#findadmiration

I'm the type of person that believe wholeheartedly
If you are going to do something,
Do it and do it well!
Learn it, know it.
There's no shame in asking how to do something while learning.
But if you're going to say you know it all,
Can do it all, and need no help,
Then walk that talk!

#adaywithdori
#randomthoughts
#windshieldtime

You can't make people that want to leave
Stay

You can't make people that want to misunderstand you
Comprehend

You can't make people that refuse to talk
Communicate
You can't make people that only want drama
Find peace

You can choose to not allow the drama get inside of you.
You can choose to love them from a distance.
You can choose to not be taken advantage of.
You can choose to remember not everything is about you.
You can choose where to put your energy.
The choices are up to you.
Choose wisely.

#adaywithdori
#youcanchoose

No one's life is all picket fences and roses.
A positive attitude is a life choice.
Somedays, having a positive attitude will be the hardest thing you'll do that day.
It also may be the best thing you do that day.
Anything is possible with a little bit of try.
Progress, not perfection.

#adaywithdori
#striveforpositivevibe

Resentment leads to bitterness, and bitterness destroys you, not the person who wronged you.
Let go of the anger.

#adaywithdori
#letitgo
#dontletthemdestroyyou

With the holidays approaching quickly, I keep seeing posts about people dreading them.
Why?

- If you get to be with family, cherish it.
- If you can't be with family, volunteer somewhere.
- Don't stress over having the "perfect" table. Eat on paper plates.
- You don't want to see certain family members. It's just dinner. Be civil. Chances are they don't want to see you either.
- Not everyone can make noon on Thursday. It's okay. It's about celebrating the holiday together, not what the calendar or clock says.
- Your child's other parent wants them? That's great. Work it out and be thankful the "other" family wants to be involved.
- You're "still" single and don't want to go to another family gathering alone? Your family doesn't care, and if they do, they shouldn't. It's your life to live.

Holidays aren't what stresses people out. It's the expectations of the "perfect family holiday."
So this year, embrace the dysfunction. Enjoy the holiday. Most importantly, make memories.

#adaywithdori
#turkeyday2017

Walk to the Talk

I'm the type of person that believes in this wholeheartedly.
If you are going to do something, do it and do it well!
Learn it, know it.
There's no shame in asking how to do something while learning.
But if you're going to say you know it all,
Can do it all,
Need no help,
Then walk that talk!

#adaywithdori
#randomthoughts
#windshieldtime

What happened to
Kindness, respect, morals, honesty, loyalty, humbleness?
Being happy for your friends and families successes? Not bitter and
spiteful out of jealousy.
Being a genuine good person—one that will make mistakes and learn
from them?
Being smart enough to know trying to keep up with the Joneses is
ridiculous?
Knowing the difference between a fake social media life and true
happiness?
Being a liar and a cheat was inexcusable?

#adaywithdori
#randomthoughts
#windshieldtime

In a conversation today, just randomly talking about holiday plans, I was asked when the kids and I do Christmas. I answered Christmas Eve. Then I was asked when does Dean have Christmas with the kids. My answer, "Christmas Eve, we all have Christmas together."

I know this shocks many, but it works best for all of us. And this little girl right here is the reason. Dean and I are friends anyway, so having holidays together isn't a big deal for us. However, making life as easy and simple as possible for the kids, grandbabies, and future grandbabies is what's important to both of us.

Don't lose sight of what's important this holiday season. Maybe you can't have holidays with your child's other parent, but at least make it as easy as possible for your children involved. You are the parent. Please remember to act like it. Our lives haven't always been this way. It's taken time, work, communication, a lot of forgiveness, and getting our priorities straight to get to where we are. Learn from us and have a great holiday season.

#adaywithdori
#randomthoughts
#windshieldtime

Before you judge a book by its cover, make sure you take the time to read through the pages.

Oftentimes I'm told I'm intimidating, too mean, too blunt, too honest, too independent. What these people don't see is that I'm caring, giving, willing to help anyone. If someone doesn't appreciate what I'll help them achieve or think they'll take advantage of me, I'll cut them out of my life without a look in the rearview mirror. I will mourn their friendship for what it was and move on.

Maybe I'm a bit "rough." I won't apologize for that part of me. Life has made me who I am. I still try my hardest to see good in everyone until they show me differently. Some say I'm bitter towards the world. That couldn't be further from the truth. I'm not bitter. I am cautious. My circle is very, very small, and there's days I feel like it will get smaller.

I hope and pray every day that this world will turn around, that people won't always try to see what they can get for free, and that hard work, dedication, loyalty, honesty, and appreciation become the rule, not the exception.

#adaywithdori
#randomthoughts
#windshieldtime

I keep reading things about "this generation," "these kids," etc. Then I see things about bad parenting, etc. I try to stay fairly neutral about parenting issues. My feelings basically are raise your kids to be productive members to society, not little assholes. If you can't, have fun supporting them the rest of your life.

Then today, I hear an advertisement on the radio that this new "Alexa" thing you can get to turn your lights on and off because you're apparently too lazy to get off the couch and will also read your child a bedtime story. Seriously?

So here are my true thoughts. Stop allowing technology to raise your kid. I read an article yesterday about toddlers being delayed in learning to talk. Thirty minutes a day of "playing on your phone" can delay your child's speech development. Why, as a parent, would you do this to your child?

Back to the basics, folks. It's not that difficult. Just do it!

#adaywithdori
#parentingisyourjob
#randomthoughts
#windshieldtime

Remember this. Do not put time and energy into someone that does not want to help themselves. It will only exhaust and disappoint you. It's tough to see potential in someone that doesn't care to better themselves or their lives. You can always circle back someday and offer help when they are ready to be helped.

#adaywithdori
#randomthoughts
#windshieldtime

Chitchatting with a wonderful friend today. She told me that she was told twice yesterday of nice things one of her boys had done recently. How refreshing that someone stepped up to compliment her child.

It seems that we all point out the negativity of life. Negativity attracts negativity. Be positive. Say nice things. Compliment your children. Say nice things about others in front of your children. Be a living example of the person you want your child to grow up to be.

#adaywithdori
#randomthoughts
#windshieldtime
#bekind

"Givers have to set limits because takers never will."

I know what having nothing is like—no hope, no belief, no passion, no money, no anything. So I'm a giver! However, over the years, I've found that limits have to be set. No matter how much you believe someone has seen how hard you've struggled to get where you are, if they don't respect you, appreciate you or value you, they will use you. This can be very hard because usually it's some of the people closest to you that become to expect you to continue to give. Remember, don't give them a hand out. Give then a hand up.

#adaywithdori
#randomthoughts
#windshieldtime

"Never forget where you came from."

As you move on to better or different things in your life, never ever lose sight of what you learned along the way and the people that taught you all you now know.

Integrity, loyalty, respect, and genuine good manners shouldn't be such a rare quality in society these days.

#adaywithdori
#randomthoughts
#windshieldtime

I see most things in life as black or white. Not much gray area for me.

- I don't believe anyone is born a bully. They are either a product of their environment or allowed to bully others. Don't raise your child to bully.
- I believe children learn by example. So be a good one.
- There are people you just aren't going to like. Be civil to them anyway.
- You might be amazing. But they'll always be someone better.
- Live your life with a purpose and let your passion shine bright.
- Everyone makes mistakes. It's being human.
- Just don't make them more than once.
- No one is above the rules or the law. So don't lie, cheat, or steal. Seriously don't, it's wrong.
- Use your manners. Always. Someone's grandma may be watching.
- Try to never burn a bridge. You may need to cross again.
- Some bridges need burnt. Light the match
- Some days your kid will be a jackass. It's even okay to tell them. Then correct their behavior.
- Be the parent first and foremost. Even once they're grown, you are always the parent.
- Never forget your "forever friends," even when you're making new friends.
- Don't be jealous. If you want what someone else has, work harder. Unless it's their spouse. You shouldn't want them. Again, it's wrong.
- Not every, successful person went to college.
- Doing nothing in a bad situation is a choice.

The way you react to situations in life says more about YOUR character than anyone else's.

#adaywithdori
#randomthoughts
#windshieldtime

Divorce/Parenting

I personally feel that all parents at one time or another together or not will intentionally or unintentionally speak badly about the other parent because we are all human beings and have bad days.

However, if you take this to the next level, put the kids in the middle. Continually belittle the other parent. Undermine the other parent's rules, rewards, or just basic parenting choices. Call your child's other parent names. Placing all of the blame on the "other" parent. You are 1000 percent in the wrong.

These are your children. Yours together.

Your job is to nurture, guide, discipline, reward, be their safe haven, the person they can tell anything to, and most of all, love them unconditionally.

They should never be told, "Don't tell," and expected to keep secrets. They should never be made to feel bad for loving the other parent.

They should never be worried about having fun or going places.

Dean and I were far from perfect divorced parents when our kids were younger. Bad choices were made. Things were said that shouldn't have been. Parenting isn't easy. Single parenting is tough. Right, wrong, or indifferent, we expected our kids to respect the other parent first and foremost always! I will never understand anyone that doesn't do this.

We were lucky none of the extended family on either side ever meddled in our child-raising days. They were our kids, not anyone else's responsibility.

I personally feel if you take the "bad mouthing" to the next level, the courts should be able to get involved. There is all this talk about mental illness in our youth and society.

Where does everyone think it starts? Children do not come out of the womb with hatred on their minds. Learned behavior can be bad or good. It all depends on the environment that surrounds the child.

#adaywithdori
#justbekind
#ifyoucantbekind
#bequiet

Super long post. Sorry.

I can't believe.

I hear this all the time when it comes to how Dean and I can get along.

I'm not going to lie. It annoys me every single time.

Last Saturday, Jimy had a trailer issue on the way to Ames. It required some quick thinking and the entire family to pitch in to get everything taken care of. Every one of us was in a different county or state. It took a little doing. This included Dean (the kids' dad, Dean) and I to drive out to Williamsburg together for one of us to drive a rig back home.

The comments made about this, even though everyone knows we get along, still amazed me.

There was an emergency. It required attention. Part of that was I needed a ride to retrieve a rig. Dean is the kids' father. He can, will, and should drop everything and help out. Seriously, why is this a foreign language to so many people?

We spent some time after our divorce not liking each other. I have to say, I'm thinking this is normal. Neither of us are perfect, and neither of us make the right decision all the time. Do I parent more than Dean? Yes. Do I dwell on that? No, why should I? My life, my choice. His life, his choice. If we spent our time being angry or hating each other for the other's choices, life would be miserable for every one of us, kids and granddaughters included. The whole entire reason we are divorced is because we didn't agree on a married life, family life, etc. Agree to disagree. Accept each other—faults and all.

I do understand with us both having businesses within the same industry and all of the kids working with us in one fashion or another, we are definitely an exception to the rule. However, we have accepted each other for the person the other has become.

If you can't get along with your ex this way, it's totally understandable. Go your separate ways. Move on and allow happiness in your children's lives.

If you can get along. Welcome to the club.

And for all you married people that judge my happy divorce, please don't, and I promise to not judge your unhappy marriage.

#adaywithdori
#wearereallyfriends
#idonthavetohatehim
#stoptheicantbelieves

I feel like Ann Landers of the construction world this week.
I am 100 percent okay with that.
Sometimes, your friends just need someone to listen while they sort
things out.

I'm not saying divorce is okay.
It's not easy.
It causes lifelong heartache for everyone involved.
However, there are times it's the only option left.

Here are few things I truly believe (you don't have to agree they're
just my opinions)
Don't stay because it's "best for the kids"
What kid wants to

- know their whole childhood was fake
- grow up in an unhappy home
- watch the fighting or the silence

Your children learn how to treat others by watching you.
Are you treating others, especially the other parent, the way you want
your child to treat others?

Mourn your marriage just like the loss of a loved one
Because it truly is a loss.
You didn't get married thinking one day you'd be divorced
Take the time you need emotionally to put closure to the dreams you
once had.

Exhaust every possible option you have to fix things.
The last thing you want to live with is regret.
But once you have, if things aren't better,
Go.
You are doing no one involved any favors by dragging things out.

Watch your words

If there are children involved.
Divorced or not, you are connected to that other parent forever,
Not just until your child is eighteen.
There are marriages, grandbaby, birthday parties, etc.
Most importantly,
Take care of you throughout whatever it is you are going through.
You can't be a good parent if you're focused on being fake or living miserable.

#adaywithdori
#divorceisntadeathsentence
#happyisbest

It saddens me to know that some divorced parents feel the need to turn their children against the "other" parent.

How low and unsecure do you have to be to want your child to hate their parent?

This says absolutely nothing about that parent that isn't there to defend themselves; however, it speaks volumes about the one doing the talking

I have been divorced for over eleven years. No, Dean and I do not and have not always seen eye to eye when it came to the kids.

But the one thing we always enforce was respect for the "other" parent. They are kids that never asked to be placed in the situation they are in. There is no right or wrong in a divorce. There is a "it didn't work out, move on."

Kids see more than you know and will make the right choices when the time is correct.

Just remember that "other parent" is your child's parent, one that YOU chose to be that parent hurting your child by making them choose to pick you over the other parent is childish and probably boarders on mental abuse

Remember you are the adult in the situation, act like it.

Also, if you do not require your children to respect the "other" parent, you are teaching them that being disrespectful is acceptable, so basically you are setting your own children up for failure in the real world.

#adaywithdori
#thekidsdidntaskforthis
#berespectful
#wrotethisin2015

There will never be a good reason to put a child in a bad situation.

Parenting is

- protecting your child at all costs
- doing the hard thing because it's the right thing
- not bad mouthing the other parent
- telling your child the truth, even when it's not what they want to hear
- not always being their friend
- making your child accountable for their actions
- loving them unconditionally (even when you don't like them much)
- listening to what your child has to say and truly hearing them
- knowing you aren't perfect and telling your child you make mistakes too
- understanding your child loves the other parent no matter how much you hate them
- requiring friends and family to be kind about the other parent or circumstances
- not expecting your child to be the adult
- showing up
- being present
- making their life better
- raising good, respectable members of society
- teaching by positive example

#adaywithdori
#leavethechildoutofit
#beagoodhuman

"Instead of teaching your kids how to be successful,
Teach them how to respond when they're unsuccessful."

We all want our kids to do their best.
We all want our kids to be successful.
We all want our kids to be the winner.

Don't forget to teach them how to be average.
Don't forget to teach them how to lose gracefully.
Don't forget they are kids.

Don't forget the winner's circle isn't what makes them successful.

#adaywithdori
#teachthemtolose
#successisntalwaysfirstplace

Best thing I've read on Facebook today:

"My kid is the kid with the not-cool parents that said no Snapchat."

As the parents,
Please, please remember.
You can say NO to anything!

It doesn't matter if Suzy, Timmy, and Bobby have it, are allowed to go, etc., etc.

Those aren't your kids.

If you don't want your kid to have a phone, download Snapchat, be on Facebook, go to that party, date or whatever else comes up, Just say no. Then stick to the no.

Do not let parent peer pressure get to you.
Your kid. Your rules.

#adaywithdori
#societysucks
#noparentpeerpressure
#yourkidyourrules

Be Your Unique Self

I'm oftentimes told that I don't realize how intimidating I can be. I find this silly and oftentimes roll my eyes at such comments. Because seriously, I don't see the reasoning behind this.

However, here are some wise words I was told long ago.

"You're not intimidating. They are intimidated. There is a difference."

Embrace your uniqueness. Be the best version of yourself. Help those you can. Encourage those in need. Stay humble. Always be kind to those deserving. Stand for what you believe in, even if you stand alone. Don't follow the crowd. Create your own path.

#adaywithdori
#oneofakind
#beagoodperson

My blunt honest truth is hard for many.

My expectations of others are often high simply because it is what I would do for them.

I'm far from perfect, but I am honest, loyal, and I love with my whole heart.

Being strong and soft is a tough combination.

At the end of the day, I feel what matters most is I was a good person that day.

But I am a person that simply just isn't for everyone. A tough pill to swallow at times, but in the end, it's okay.

#adaywithdori
#iamnotforeveryone
#beunique
#beyourself

No one should compare their journey to anyone else's. However, if you feel the need to compare, at least don't one-up anyone.

I personally am fine with the fact I did not go to college. Also, I'm happy for you that you did, and I'm not going to criticize you for not being self-employed.

I'm okay driving an '89 freightliner.

I'm thrilled that you have a newer nicer truck, but I'm not going to ask you about your payments.

I love my little house out in the middle of nowhere. No, I don't want to remodel or add on. If you want a giant house, that's great. I'll come visit and take off my shoes on your expensive carpet.

I personally don't care what my kids think of my career choice. This career raised them well as a 100 percent single-parent household. I'm glad your kids are not embarrassed by your job either. Because honestly, no child should be so entitled that they have an opinion.

Yep, I'm divorced. I'm fine with it because it was the best decision for myself and my kids. I'm glad your marriage has lasted twenty plus years. I won't mention how bitter and miserable you seem.

Seriously, some things are better left unsaid. This was an actual conversation. Well, the parts about my life. I truly do not care how my friends live their lives. It must be unbelievably exhausting to be so worried about someone else's life that you are absolutely no part of.

#adaywithdori
#dontbeaoneupper
#behappy
#nocomparision

Not everyone thinks like you. Or would make the choices or sacrifices you have to get to where you are right this minute in your life. It's okay. Continue your journey. Life isn't about what someone else might do or not do. It's about what you will do. It's about seeing your future for what it will be and working hard every day to get where you belong in life.

#adaywithdori
#createyourlife
#neverslowyourhustle

A DAY WITH DORI

I heard it again this morning.
We all say it.
When someone says, "How've ya been?"
You respond with, "Same old, same old."
Today my friend, Deb, said, "Just going through the motions."

Why?
Why aren't people living? Loving life? Enjoying themselves?

Life is short. It could all change in the blink of an eye.
Take chances.
Try and fail. Take a trip.
Quit a job.
Start a business.
Just stop "going through the motions."

#adaywithdori
#liveyourlife
#dreambig

Do not ever allow someone make you question your own worth.

The power is in your hands, not in anyone else's.

Their silence could be a huge blessing.
Silence speaks loudly.

Listen closely.
You are hearing everything they aren't saying.

#adaywithdori
#dontgivesomeonepower
#silencespeaksloudly

There are times walking away speaks louder than any words ever could.
Pick your battle.
Do not allow them to drag you into their drama.
Peace of mind is a beautiful choice.
It's your life. Never lose sight of that.

#adaywithdori
#bestrong
#justwalkaway

Don't let anyone tell you to slow your hustle to fit their life.

Go after what YOU want. Live YOUR life. The haters will always hate.
The nonbelievers can watch and wish. The skeptics will ask you why,
then they will ask you how.
Find your why, your happiness, your reasons.
But never ever slow your hustle.

What if we just told people what was actually going on in our lives?
Instead of protecting the ones that treat their families poorly.
Instead of being embarrassed because of what someone close to us
has done.
Instead of worrying about what society might think.
Instead of being "hopeful" no one will find out.

Just tell it like it is.

I've always been a firm believer in
If you don't want someone to know,
Don't do it.

I don't mean only talk badly about other people.
I don't mean constantly complain about a family member.
I don't mean be overly dramatic.
I don't mean expect others to pick a side.

Everywhere you go,
Big town,
Small town,
Work,
School,
Family gatherings,
Kids' sports.
Hobbies,

There will always be rumors.

What if when someone asked you how life was,
You actually told them?

#adaywithdori
#justtellitlikeitis
#whyprotectthosethatdontcare
#justspeakthetruth

Not everyone will agree with you.
How you live your life or raise your kids,
What career you've chosen,
Your choice in a relationship or lack of a relationship,
It's okay.
You don't need their approval.
You have the ability to succeed without them.
No matter what position they hold in your life,
Success comes from within YOU!

#adaywithdori
#riseabove

You will never scare the right people.
The right people in your life will be proud and supportive that you are whole all by yourself.
They will know that they are in your life because you truly want them there.

The people that you scare,
Those are the people that don't understand self-strength,
Those are the people that will always NEED to be needed,
You'll be able to easily spot them.
They're the ones telling everyone how great they are.
Their ego and arrogance will enter a room before they ever cross the threshold.

Do not allow their criticism of you effect your day,
For remember, you would never seek their advice.

#adaywithdori
#bewholealone
#justbeyou
#dontworryaboutothersfears

I see so much on social media about empowered women should empower others.
I wholeheartedly agree with this.

I also wholeheartedly believe you should do so quietly.
You don't need to tell the whole world you have empowered someone.

Empowering someone isn't about your recognition.
It is about changing that person's life.
If your personal story or words of encouragement can change someone's life for the better.

You are an amazing person for sharing this part of your life.

Lead by example.
Always be your best self.

#adaywithdori
#straightenhercrownquietly

Don't live to be better than anyone but yourself.

- Everyone can strive to be a better person today than they were yesterday.
- Being better doesn't mean better than your coworker, neighbor, friend, or workout buddy.
- It doesn't mean you need to be a better parent than anyone else.
- Just better than you were yesterday.

Don't compare yourself to anyone other than the reflection in the mirror.
We are all winging this life thing, work, home, family, kids.
Be YOUR best, not anyone else's.

#adaywithdori
#beyourbest

A long talk yesterday with a great friend about random things lead to this. Sorry, long post.

We started talking about how other women perceive each other, how judgmental they truly can be.

How they are going to silently judge your hair, clothes, shoes, makeup, fingernails, etc. Now before you say, "I don't do that," (I agree, not everyone does) but I also bet at some point, everyone has.

You cannot stop someone from judging you. What you can do is be so confident in yourself. Their silent criticism doesn't affect you. And seriously, they just may be so caught up in their own struggles that they don't notice you are a hot mess that day.

Is self-confidence easy? Absolutely not. It is a huge mental struggle you play against yourself. Stop playing that game. We are our own worst critics and our own worst enemies.

You do YOU!

Ask yourself some tough questions:

- Are you a genuinely good person?
- I'm not saying perfect. I'm saying a good, honest person. Do you take care of your own? Don't steal, cheat, and lie. Don't jump on the drama train, etc.
- Do you have a work ethic? Even if it's not the career you want, but it pays the bills now as you work towards the career you love.
- Is your house clean enough? I don't mean spotless. I mean lived in. Mine is a mess six out of seven days a week. But it's clean. (Thanks, Courtney)
- Could you be healthier, skinnier, toner? Couldn't we all? Are you working towards these goals no matter how slowly?

No one has the right to judge you. You have an obligation to yourself to not care what they say or think. Every person in this world could use some improvement somewhere along the way. Life is a journey, not a destination.

I used to be the first part of this quote. I was a teenage mother. I was a mother of four by the age of twenty-four. Had weight problems on and off. Divorced at thirty-one or thirty-two. Started my own trucking business at thirty-five years old as a single mom. Let my boys ride rough stock, etc. Believe me, I have been judged seven ways to Sunday. All of these things will take a toll on you mentally if you let them.

Now I'm the last part of this quote. I'm far from perfect. I still struggle with my weight. I'm still a single mom, now with three businesses of my own. My boys still rodeo and do rather well. I am independent to a fault.

The difference between the first and last is I stopped caring what others thought. When I go to sleep at night, I know I did okay that day—maybe not perfect but okay. My bills are paid. My kids are loved. I may have looked like I fell out of the goodwill box that day, but I'm okay with that. I'm not here to impress anyone but me.

#adaywithdori #doyou #dontbejudgy

Ran into an acquaintance today.
After idle chit chat,
I was told "Well, you don't seem too upset about things."
Meaning Dean's death
Here's the deal:

- Everyone grieves differently.
- I chose to try to get through every day in a positive manner.
- I have businesses to run.
- I have children to help.

There are so many things I could point out. But here is what I know to be true. Dean would not want anyone sad about his death. He never allowed me to use him as a crutch to get through life. He expected me to take care of things no matter what life throws at me.

Please do not ever judge someone's grief by outward appearances. I miss him every minute of every day. As much as no one wants to hear this,
Life will go on.
It's hard.
It's sad.
It's not fair.
But it's the hand we've been dealt.

#adaywithdori
#playthecardsyourdealt

"You're intimidating."
I hear this so often.
It's annoying.
I'm just me.

Yes,
I'm strong, independent, stubborn, blunt, honest, and a whole lot of
other things.
I'm also kind, caring, giving, helpful, and a whole lot of other things.

I am the way I am because life made me this way.

Every one of us has a choice while facing everyday decisions or once-
in-a-lifetime tragedies.

My focus over the years has always been to "do what needs done."
I had kids to raise.
I had a business to run.
I screwed up a lot in both areas.
I tried to never dwell on it.
I learned and I moved forward.

You can too!

Never waste your time being jealous of what someone else has become,
Whether it's a career, relationship, or a personal achievement.
You have no idea what it took for them to get there.

Instead, focus on where YOU want to go in life
What obstacles do you need to be bigger then? Do you want a different career? Do you want to have better relationships with others? Do
you want a better relationship with yourself? Only you can achieve
these things for yourself. Focus on what YOU want and need.

Please stop letting others intimidate you. Please stop being jealous of
where or what others have in life.

Put your energy into yourself and your future.

Most of all, don't be jealous of a story that you only came into 3/4 of the way through the book.

#adaywithdori
#imnotintimidating
#idontgetjealousy
#focusonyou

That reflection in the mirror can do anything.
Don't limit yourself because someone else said you couldn't.
Society shouldn't dictate who you become.
You need no one but yourself to complete you.
Take that first big scary step to believe in yourself.
Don't limit yourself, don't settle for mediocre, don't just be
LIVE!!

#behappy
#oneofakind
#neversettle

A DAY WITH DORI

If you don't have self-made happiness from the inside out,

Marking things off your "grocery list" isn't going to change that.

#adaywithdori
#choosehappy
#lifeisntalist

The choice is yours.
You can stay bitter and angry for the rest of your days over a situation
you can't change
Or you can decide you are worth more than that.
Forgive those that don't deserve forgiveness.
Not because they deserve it
Because you do

#adaywithdori
#forgiveandmoveon
#ididntsayforget
#youareworthit

Do not ever compare yourself to anyone else.
There is no need in life to be jealous of anyone or anything.
If you don't like where you are in life or the person life has made you become,
Change!
Don't blame anyone or make excuses for where you are at in life.
Take ownership and make the necessary changes.

#adaywithdori
#beyou
#oneofakind

A DAY WITH DORI

I was asked for advice today from a young girl that's been through quite a bit in her few years on this earth.

Here's the deal, people:

You should not ever judge others.
No snide comments.
No talking behind someone's back.
If you wouldn't say it to them, never say it about them.
Be better than that.

- Growing up is hard.
- Being a young adult is hard.
- Making mistakes is hard.
- Having people you thought were your friends just to find out they aren't is hard.

No one on this earth knows what you are going through.

Although it's easy to say and extremely hard to accomplish,
Ignore the haters.
Just walk away.
You and only you know what's best for your life.

Never refuse to do what's best for the reflection in the mirror.
It is the most important person in your life.

#adaywithdori
#focusonyou
#hatersgonnahate

"You work too much."
I hear this often.
It is 110 percent true.
I'm okay with it.
Self-employed people have to thoroughly enjoy what they do or it is
just another job.

I have never wanted to be someone that simply "lived" for the weekend.

I've always wanted to enjoy my life every day.
I don't. That's fairytale talk.
But it's close.

I once had a job that made me physically sick to go to.
I once lived somewhere I absolutely hated.
I drove a five-speed pink escort wagon for a lot of years.

I know the feeling of being unsure how I'd pay for groceries,
Worrying where Christmas present money would come from,
Praying I'd have enough to pay the mortgage and gas money for the
kid's next rodeo.

This isn't a post for attention or a "You've done well."
It is simply a reminder that where you are doesn't have to be where
you stay.
Hard work and determination will get you further ahead.

While I do work too much,
I also created myself a life that I don't need to "get away from."
I don't dread Monday morning.
I don't live for Friday afternoon.
I absolutely love going home and staying there.

Work too hard.
Be stubborn.
Create a life you love.

You'll never please everyone.
Just worry about pleasing yourself.

#adaywithdori
#createalifeyoulove
#tuneoutthenaysayers

I received a message Sunday after a post I made.
It made my day.
Honestly, it has made my whole week.
This one simple message from an amazing girl.
I don't try to be inspiring.
I am just me.
I'm too blunt.
I'm too honest. (Yes, it is a thing.)
I'm too independent.
I'm too black and white.
I'm too much of something for many.

However, I'm not changing.

I've fought hard to become the person I am.
Never underestimate the light you can bring to someone's day by
simply sending them a message to say, "Keep being you."
She may have sent me this message to tell me I'm inspiring.
Little does she know, she did the inspiring on this day.

#adaywithdori
#keepbeingyou
#bekindbeafriend
#simplemessagechangelives

Do not lose sight of yourself
Even when others don't appreciate your kindness.
Never let someone else's actions dictate your behavior.
Always be true to yourself first. Don't let someone make you unkind.

#adaywithdori
#neverregretbeingyou
#dontletthemruinyou

Negativity is everywhere.
If it's time to walk away from the negative people in your life, the ones that bring you down,
Do it!
It doesn't mean you don't still consider them great friends or family.
It means your mindset is so much more important than their opinion.
You are only going to be as successful in life as the people you surround yourself with.
So take a long look.
Are you surrounded by positivity, inspiring people that want to watch you succeed or are you allowing people to bring you down?
The ones with the "you'll never be able to do that" attitude,
The "you'll never succeed without me" people,
I've been told these things.
With my crazy, stubborn, sassy attitude,
It was just the push for me to say,

"Watch this"

#adaywithdori
#oneofakind
#createyourfuture
#embracetheuniqueinyou
#neverslowyourhustle

I was invited to sit in on a conference call meeting this morning.

Topic:
Empowering Women

I'm positive. Most people understand I'm a very outside-the-box thinker.

This is my take away from this morning:

Being an empowering woman
Should NOT equal bashing men

If you want to be good at what you do,
I encourage you do strive to be the best in your field.

If you want to be influential to others,
I encourage you to do so with all that you are.

If you want to be taken seriously in your career of choice,
Be a positive, hard-working, non-judgmental, good-at-your job person

If you need to put others down, especially men, to get your point across that you are an empowering woman,
In my opinion, you've missed the point of the topic.

There is nothing empowering

- about putting others down
- about saying we'll show those men how to do it
- about thinking you're better then someone else

I've heard about this empowering women thing for the last few years While I believe the meaning behind it is genuine and was put in place to remind women they can do for themselves.

Let's not forget it's 2020. Why are you choosing to have empowering women meetings and not empowering people meetings?

You can't want to be treated equally
At the same time separate yourselves.

If you want respect from men, especially in the workplace,

- do your job
- ask for help if needed, then learn what you've been taught
- dress for your career of choice
- do not ever pull "I'm a girl" card
- give respect to get respect
- be professional at all times regardless of your career choice

You'll always have chosen a few men that can't handle your presence,
kill 'em with kindness.

The good ole boys club will always be a "thing" you don't need to
choose to attend.
Oftentimes they do things to see if they can get a response.
Smile, nod, wave, and go on with what you're doing.

Never forget if you are in a position to empower others,
Do so with grace and dignity.

I've never understood the
"I'm a woman hear me roar,"
Especially at work.

I'm much more of a
I'm a person
I'll just do my job. It's what they pay me for.

#adaywithdori
#justempowerpeople
#itsnotmenversuswomen
#justworktogether

Remember to not let the outside world influence your inner self.
It's your journey. Live it your way.

#adaywithdori
#yourjourney

I work A LOT!
Everyone in my life knows this.
Just the other day I was asked,
"Why?"
Why do I work like I do?
It's simple. I was once told I couldn't do it all on my own.
Well, you just don't tell a stubborn, hard-headed, sassy girl something so silly.
So no, I'm not done "proving my point"
Because I'm creating a life I absolutely love!
Can you say the same?

#adaywithdori
#neverslowyourhustle
#createyourfuture

The choice ultimately is truly yours.
I've had not-so-good circumstances.
I've made poor, very poor choices.
But the day I decided to no longer live that way was the day my life changed for the better.
It's not perfect, far from it.
But I choose every day to make the best decisions I can for my family, my businesses, my faith, and myself.
Your future truly, truly is in your own hands.

#adaywithdori
#createyourfuture

No one should fall into a pattern of following others.
Stand on your own two feet.
Do your own thing.
There is a lot to be said for being independent and living your life on your terms.

#adaywithdori
#dontbeasheep
#beawiseoldwolf

Learning to be alone is the best gift you can give yourself.
No need to depend on anyone.
Depending on others sets you up for unrealistic expectations.
It makes you needy and allows you to settle for far less than you deserve.
Allow yourself to be GOOD on your own, so when God puts that "just right person" in your life, you can be GREAT together.

#adaywithdori
#loveyouralonetime
#learntobegood
#thenbegreat

"It's not the road we take, it's how we take the road."
In this crazy world, it's easy to get caught up in all the negativity that happens every day.
Don't do this.
It's exhausting.
It's mentally tough.
It's stressful.
My life is far from perfect.
I work too much, worry about my family and our future more than needed.
Do I wish every day that my life was different, better, easier?
Heck ya, I do.
Then I reflect on where I started, where I am. And where I'm going.
Count my blessings and move on.

#adaywithdori
#oneofakindkindalife
#nodoovers
#onetimeoffer

A DAY WITH DORI

Once in a while, you look around and realize life has thrown you into
a competition you never asked for.

Step out.
Back off.
Stop competing.

You don't have to make it a production.
Simply and silently step out.
Then proceed in silence and create the life you're longing for.

#adaywithdori
#dontplaythegame
#stepoutoftherace

Your best
Will never look like anyone else's best.
Guess what? That's okay.

Your best is simply that
Giving your best of yourself to yourself and your commitments.

You don't have to be to a breaking point.
Just do what you can for today.

#adaywithdori
#giveyouyourbest
#behappy
#behealthy

It's not a competition.
Just be a mom.
Love them.
Feed them.
Let them make mistakes.
Love them harder.

Just do your best,
Whatever your best looks like that day.

Believe me when I say your best

- isn't the amount of money spent
- isn't if you allowed them to play that travel sport
- isn't the newest electronics
- isn't the name brand clothes

o It's time.
o It's allowing them to talk to you without judgement.
o It's being in the stands whenever possible.
o It's being a true part of their life.

But seriously, hire someone to teach them math.

#adaywithdori
#dontbesohardonyourself
#justlovethem

"I've learned
Two people can look at the exact same thing and see something completely different."

Just because someone doesn't see things the same way you do, it doesn't make them wrong. It makes their opinion different than yours.

As a society, it seems we crave the "approval" of others to justify our life choices.
Why?
Society isn't raising your children, paying your bills, working towards your career goals, etc.
It's okay to agree to disagree.
Respect each other for being their own person.

#adaywithdori
#itsokaytobedifferent
#beyourownperson

I had an interesting conversation last night with an elderly gentleman as we walked back to our vehicles after a rodeo.

We both had went to the rodeo alone. I had a two-hour drive, he had about fifteen minutes.

He thought it was amazing I was by myself. He says, "Seems like everyone runs in packs these days. How can a person know what they want if they're always following someone else around?"

There is so much truth in those words. I enjoy my alone time more than most people.

Learn to love your own company. Go out to dinner, a movie, whatever you want. Step out of your comfort zone. You may be surprised with how much you enjoy yourself.

#adaywithdori
#loveyouralonetime
#beyourownperson

The best friendships are with people you haven't talked to in a while. But when they hear something rather unpleasant said about your success, they pick up the phone, call, and talk with you for an hour just to remind you exactly how far you've came.

I've never understood jealousy. It truly seems like a waste of energy. Don't get me wrong. I'm jealous of plenty of things in my life: retired people, parents that can get to every kid event, skinny people that don't have to try to be skinny, etc. I also know for me to have these things, it requires effort—effort that I'm willing to put forth.

The jealousy I don't understand is the talking nasty, backstabbing, two-faced, want-to-ruin-your-life people. Why? What exactly does it gain someone to be so downright jealous that they would want to ruin someone's life?

In my thoughts, if they put that amount of energy into making their life better, they would be incredibly successful at whatever direction they choice to take in life.

So for now, I'll cherish my amazing friends, continue to build my businesses, value my relationship with my family, and realize that I obviously did some amazing things along the way because no one is jealous of a loser.

#adaywithdori
#workonyou
#jealousyisugly

Self-Action

It's up to you to decide where you choose to put your effort.

If you're unsure if your efforts are appreciated,

Simply take a step back,
Stop "doing" for someone,
See where that road leads you.
Will they notice?
Will they be upset?
Will they change?

It may be time to make some decisions for what's best for you
Or
You may not always be happy and content being the "giver"
While the "taker" continues to take your kindness for granted.

Some of the hardest lessons learned
Are the lessons lived the hard way.
Oftentimes this stings the most because you'd not take advantage of them the way they may be taking advantage of you.

Once you put this all together,
It could be time to put more effort towards the people that would be grateful for a drop of water.

#adaywithdori
#chosewhereyoureffortsgo
#beappreciated
#lovethemfromadistance

You have no idea what someone has had to overcome to be where they are at in life.

Do not belittle someone for having feelings.

If your feelings have been hurt by someone you care about, explain yourself like an adult in your out-loud words. The other person may be unaware you're upset.

If it continues, well then, remove yourself from a situation where others don't respect your feelings.

#adaywithdori
#neverletsomeoneinvalidateyou
#stateyourfeelings
#explainlikeanadult

We all have toxic people in our past. There is a reason they are in the past. Just leave them there,
Behind you where they belong.

It doesn't matter if you're lonely or if they are your "go to" for something.
Learn to be comfortable being alone.
Teach yourself how to do those things without the toxicity of others.

If you allow yourself to get drag back down, it will continue to be harder to pull yourself back up.
Rip the Band-Aid off and walk away from anything that is toxic for your heart and soul.

#adaywithdori
#dontdrinkthepoison

Be the best you, you can be.
Don't concern yourself with what others think of you.
Life is hard enough trying to take care of yourself, your family, your
pets, your job, along with any other responsibilities you may have.
If you allow negative thoughts to affect how you feel about yourself,
you are wasting precious time and energy. Do not—I repeat—do not
do that to yourself.
Life is not a competition. You have nothing to prove to anyone except
yourself.

If you want more out of life, figure it out, work harder, go back to
school, grab an unrealistic opportunity. Do it for YOU!
Life is what you make it. Give out the vibe you want in return.

See yourself as the tiger you are, not as the domestic cat the world
tries to conform you to.

#adaywithdori
#beatiger

Twice today I was told,
"I love your Facebook posts. They are so real and in your face, in a good way."

Which left me standing there thinking I haven't posted much lately.
I haven't had much of anything positive to say.
I like positive.
I like upbeat.
I like real.
I know life isn't always picket fences and roses.
It is strictly what you make of it.

However, lately, people suck.

Don't get me wrong. I have some absolutely great, amazing, wonderful people in my life, and I know it. I appreciate these people every minute of every day or at least try.

Then there are the rude, disrespectful, selfish people. The ones that strictly just want what they want with no regard to anyone else. The ones that appear not have much in the way of morals, standards, or integrity. I do not allow these people to get me down or keep me down. However, because of them, I've found it hard to post anything positive lately. Basically, what I'd like to say isn't worth my time or effort. The takers wouldn't understand it.

I watched people around town today with a sheer lack of respect for others. All I could think was, *Thank goodness I'm not you.*

Here's my best advice today:

Think before you act.
Put yourself in other's shoes before you make decisions that could affect anyone else besides yourself.
Be grateful for good people.
Do not take advantage of anyone's kindness.

Use common sense.
Don't be a taker.

#adaywithdori
#youarentbetterthenanyone

I've recently seen many posts saying I thought so and so was a true friend. Then you find out they aren't.
Hopefully, this little deal I found on Facebook will help you decide next time how to react to such "friends."

Not everyone that comes into your life is meant to stay forever. Some are just passing through. Cherish the memories you've made. Remember the lessons you've learned. Allow God to show who stays and who goes.

Also, remember this. Some of the best friends you'll ever have aren't the people you talk to everyday. They are the ones you know are a simple phone call away when you need them.
Life is busy. Respect everyone's amount of crazy busy and proceed from there.

#adaywithdori
#noteveryoneismeanttostay
#allowgodtoshowyou

I was told recently that there's no way life is as good as I portray it on Facebook. Here's my thoughts on that.

Life is what you make it. I could complain because a truck broke down, a driver overslept, the job that was to be all day lasted two hours or that I'm having a bad day because I'm a girl (somedays that's the only reason) or because someone I thought was more of a friend than a business associate and threw me under a bus for their benefit.

Or that I understand why some species eat their young (give me a break, single mom of four kids, it has its days) I could go on and on.

But I choose to be positive, look into the future to see what needs changed. Some doors have closed in my past, some that I thought never would, some that I didn't think would the way they did. But EVERY closed door has given me a HUGE opportunity to a bigger, brighter future. The wide open fields I see have no west fence line, just greener pasture.

#adaywithdori
#lifeiswhatyoumakeit

A DAY WITH DORI

People grow and evolve daily.

- Some people grow with you.
- Some don't.
- Sometimes when the lesson is over, you or they move on.

Not everyone is meant to continue your journey with you.

Maybe they helped you regain yourself.
Maybe they taught you who not to be.

Whatever their purpose,
It is okay that you cherish what that relationship taught you.
Move on gracefully with your head held high.

#adaywithdori
#lifeisajourney
#cherishthememories

You show people your priorities.
You don't tell them.

Anyone can tell a good story.
***********The bigger question is*************

Can you live the same way you speak?
Watch how people live.
Be observant of what isn't being said.

#adaywithdori
#prioritiesrevealed

If you want people to respect you, you first must be a person worth respecting.

Don't tell people what you'll do.
Show them.

Don't expect people to give to you.
Earn it.

No amount of words will ever outtalk the fact you are a slacker.

#adaywithdori
#notafanoflaziness
#workhardbeforeyouplayhard

More money won't solve your problems if you have poor spending habits.

A relationship will never "complete" you unless you know how to be happy alone.

Learn to love the life you live.

Build a strong foundation. Then add on.

#adaywithdori
#beyourfoundation

Be an eagle. Conquer the world in silence.

We all have those people we think are our friends. However, as soon as you are successful in your career, personal life, parenting, hobbies, etc., their true colors shine through. It's okay. These kind of people are not "forever" friends. Do not dwell on their selfish behavior. Be grateful for the time spent with them. Enjoy the memories. Understand their time in your life, while enjoyable, wasn't meant to last forever.

#adaywithdori
#soarlikeaneagle

As I scroll through the ole Facebook, I notice all kinds of things:
Happy, sad, funny, depressing, etc.
If I don't like it, I scroll past.
I honestly see no reason to comment something negative on a post or unfriend someone because of Facebook.
However, I do wonder if the people posting on Facebook about how bad their life is, using profanity, talking bad about their bosses or job, etc.
Then in a few hours make a post about why don't I have friends?
I can't find a job?
No one will help me out.
Well, nope.
No one probably wants to help you because they will be bashed on Facebook in your next post.
If you want to be treated with respect,
Have respect.
I'm not saying don't have an opinion.
I'm saying be mindful that someone's grandma could be reading your profanity-ridden opinion.

#adaywithdori
#justhaverespect

Just think about it:

- It takes less effort to tell the truth than to remember a lie.
- It takes less effort to admit mistakes than hide them.

If you continue to always do the wrong thing but try to explain why
it was okay,
People eventually will just stop listening.
Everyone deserves a chance to right a wrong once in a while.
Learning from that wrong and not writing a book of excuses is what
will make people believe you aren't going to repeat the process.

Life is a learning experience
Only if you're willing to learn.

#adaywithdori
#dontwasteenergy
#dotherightthing

I will be your biggest cheerleader.
I will support and encourage every step you take in the right direction.
I can be a listening ear, a giver of advice or just be there so you aren't alone.

But if you pull the "poor me," "why me," "bad things always happen to me" card,
I'm out.
Stop trying to seek attention and sympathy for situations you put yourself into.
Every person in this world goes through unpleasant situations.
Some are just downright hard and life-changing.
You aren't the only one.
I promise.

#adaywithdori
#dontplayvictim
#beyourownsavior

Not sure where I originally read this, but I saved it on my phone. It originally said, "Women," but I don't live or work in a women's world. My world in all aspects is male-dominated. Worry about your very own progress and less about the competition.

"People putting other people down is like telling the world you are more worried about your COMPETITION than your own progress."

#adaywithdori
#workonyou
#progressnotperfection

Your happiness is not anyone else's responsibility.
Your happiness comes from within you.

Also, you are not responsible for making anyone else happy.
Their happiness is their own job.

Please do not put so much burden on someone you want in your life.
Find your own happy and allow them to add to your happiness.

#adaywithdori
#findyourhappy
#happinesscomesfromwithin

If you can't speak your thoughts out loud,
Check your tribe.
With the right people, you should be able to speak the blunt, honest truth.
If it offends them,
You're probably with the wrong people.

#adaywithdori
#donttiptoe
#speakyourthoughts

Bring effort.

Effort

- indicates interest
- shows passion
- means commitment

These things ensure no time is being wasted.

That the feelings you have for these:

- career
- relationship
- hobby

Are genuine.

Effort is a huge part of life.

If you have no desire to put in the effort,
Don't be upset with the results.

#adaywithdori
#bringeffort

It is 100 percent okay to say,

"I'm the problem, and I need to take the time needed to fix me."

You aren't the problem because you're:

- broken
- weak
- selfish

Or anything else you can make up in your own mind.

Maybe it's simply being overwhelmed by life.
Maybe you just aren't where you thought you'd be.

Maybe you're disappointed in some life choices you made.

Maybe you're grieving a loss.

Maybe you put trust in people you shouldn't have and need to rebalance.

The focus shouldn't be:
"I'm the problem."

The focus should be the following:

- These are the steps I'm going to take to fix the problem.
- I'm taking accountability for me.
- I want to learn how to fix this and move forward.
- I need to heal me.

You are responsible for your actions.
Take accountability where it is needed.

#adaywithdori
#sometimesimtheproblem
#taketimetorefocus

Everyone

- is busy
- doesn't know how
- doesn't know anyone
- doesn't want to "put themselves out there"

There are a million excuses for everything. Do not allow those excuses kill your opportunity to success.

#adaywithdori
#ditchtheexcuses
#beourownsuccess

Happiness and peace come from within YOU.
You can want a new everything:
Life, career, house, friends, etc.
But what makes you think you'll be happy with something new if you haven't been happy with what you already have?
Always remember the grass is the greenest where you water it the most.

#adaywithdori
#randomthoughts
#wateryourgrass

Take the time YOU need to heal

It doesn't matter what the situation was that hurt you.

Although it's absolutely necessary to continue through everyday life.

There is no time limit on healing.

Take your alone time.
Take a different job.
Take up a new hobby.

Just remember to put your demons behind you before you move forward.

The new people in your life should never be punished for something someone in your past did.

- Your new best friend shouldn't be criticized for what a different friend did.
- Your new relationship should never suffer from a past love.
- Your new boss shouldn't have to prove he isn't like your old boss.

You will run across people all throughout different phases in your life that will let you down.

Heal from those disappointments.

Then continue on with life.

You'll never be totally free from disappointment.

Only you can determine how much control those disappointments have over you.

#adaywithdori
#taketimetoheal
#leavethepastbehindyou

I can't tell you how many times I've had someone say to me,
"I wish I could tell them how I feel. But it'll just make things worse."

I truly understand this way of thinking.
I've done so on more than one occasion.

However, have you ever stopped to think

That the person you're concerned about "keeping peace" with
Doesn't care how their actions affect you?

Perhaps they don't realize what they're doing.
Although, I truly believe they know.
They also know you'll "get over it"
Or maybe because you've never said anything. They don't believe it's
an issue.

It's your job to maintain your own mental peace.
If that means speaking your mind,
Please do so.
Let the chips fall where they may.

Never forget the peace within you is not only important
But absolutely necessary.

#adaywithdori
#keepthepeacewithinyou

Everyone has bad days
The "why me" days
The "I can't" days
The "I don't want to" days
The "everyone is against me" days

Some will choose to live those days over and over every day forever, waiting for someone to "rescue" them, to save them from their own misery. These people will limit their beliefs every single day for the rest of forever.

Others will realize that only they can change their path. They will grow from failures and setbacks. They will find the positivity in at least something every day. They will become better. They will empower themselves with their own thoughts every single day for the rest of forever.

#adaywithdori
#empoweringbeliefs
#donotlimityourself

Your education, financial status, and material things are important to support the lifestyle you desire.
However, those things will never make you better than anyone else.
Don't confuse what you "have" with "who you are."

#adaywithdori
#dontthinkyourbetter

—Sometimes risking everything is the only thing worth doing.—

People often say,
"I wish I had _____"

When I hear that,
I always wonder,

Why didn't you?

If you allow fear to hold you back,
You'll never move forward.

If something doesn't work out for you,
So what?
At least you wouldn't go through the rest of your life thinking,
If only I had tried.

- Start that business.
- Take that class.
- Quit that job.
- Move to that state.
- Ask that girl out.
- Begin that hobby.
- Buy that house.
- Call that old friend.

Life is short.
There should be no room for the
I wish
I should have
If only

There should be

- I took this class once.

- I moved to this great neighborhood.
- I met this amazing guy.
- I learned this cool hobby.
- I started my own business.

Life is full of opportunities every single day.

You can choose to take a risk and start a new path
Or
Stay in your comfort zone and possibly live with regret

The choice is yours and yours alone.

As my boys would say,
"You gotta risk it for the biscuit."

#adaywithdori
#takethatrisk
#sometimeriskiswellworthit
#dontlivewithregret

No one is perfect.
We all need to fix our reflection from time to time.
The important part is taking the time to admit we need fixing.
Then to follow through with the steps needed to fix yourself.

#adaywithdori
#fixyourreflection

Stop seeing the good in people.
Start seeing what they show you.

I'll always say, "Be kind."
I'll also always tell you to be smart.

Sometimes you have to stop seeing what you want someone to be
To start seeing who they truly are.

Step back.
Look at the big picture.
Really see what they are showing you.

Then decide if it's for you or not.

#adaywithdori
#startseeingwhattheyshowyou
#lookatthebigpicture

I'll always be the person that says

1. Tell them how you feel.
2. Use your out-loud words.
3. Have an adult conversation.

However,
Sometimes you need to use your judgment.

- Will this person be open-minded enough to understand?
- Can this person comprehend they aren't always right?
- Does this person realize everyone sees a situation differently?

I'm a firm believer that the more "shit" you've been through in life
Makes it easier to see someone else's struggle.

Everyone has struggles,
Some worse than others

Oftentimes those who've struggled the hardest are the most understanding individuals you'll ever meet.

#adaywithdori
#knowyouraudience
#dontstressoverothers

If you allow yourself to stay mad at someone, it's just wasted energy.
Thank the Good Lord for showing you their true colors.
Then take all the time you need to heal and move on. Never forget to
move on. Being mad forever just allows someone else to have power
over you.

#adaywithdori
#truecolorswillcomeout
#dontwasteyourenergy

Relationship Advice

I've been working with some new-to-me contractors the last month or so. Relationships always get brought up. I'm unsure why they seek my advice. Seriously I've been single since 2004. However, the one thing I notice is this: Most of the wives, fiancés, girlfriends, and potential girlfriends these guys tell me about all have one thing in common. The guy is never spending enough money on them, taking them out enough, buying them enough nice presents, etc.

Now first off, I'm not defending the fact that these guys could be spending all their money on beer or their own hobbies, etc.

The one thing I don't understand is: if these women want to have nicer things, go more places, etc., why are they upset some guy isn't doing this for them? The days of one-household incomes are in the past. If you want to go on a great vacation, save up and take your family, movies, dinner, whatever. He doesn't owe you these things.

He owes you respect, affection, loyalty, selflessness, love, etc. He should open doors for you, take care of household "guy" stuff. Be proud to show you off when you have messy hair and no makeup. Send you messages in the middle of the day so you know you're on his mind. That's what he "owes" you.

#adaywithdori

I have a really good friend that calls me a few times a month wanting relationship advice.

For. The. Same. Problem. Every. Time.

Here is the deal: If you continue not making changes, you've created the situation you're living in.

Good or bad.

If you are waiting around for the people in your life to acknowledge their poor behavior that you've allowed to happen continuously,

You, my friend, will be waiting forever.

Let people know you aren't okay with how they are treating you if you want to see a change.

If you choose to not communicate, please do not be upset with the outcome.

#adaywithdori
#choosechange

Occupational hazard of my job some days is being the "Ann Landers" of construction. Here are things I find myself repeating:

- If she is looking to be saved, let her save herself. Then she can call you.
- If you're lonely, it's okay. Learn to be alone and like it.
- If you are posting things on Facebook such as: Where's the party tonight? I can't wait to get drunk tonight. Etc. Do not complain you can't find a "good girl" because she is looking for a man that can handle everyday stress. Not someone that deals with life like an eighteen-year-old.
- If you're upset she isn't going to "hang out" with you, try asking her on an actual date.
- Do not tell her about the "other girls" you're talking to.
  - She doesn't want to hear it.
  - You've just proven you're either unfaithful or scared to be alone.

No one wants to be a fill-in until you find something better.

- If you really want a relationship with her, be the man you'd want your daughter to date.

#adaywithdori
#itsnotalltruckdriving

I did my "Ann Landers of the construction world" duties today.

This is always my first bit of advice.
Communicate
Like an adult
Have a conversation with your out-loud words.
If you can't talk to your significant other about an issue in your relationship,
Why are you in the relationship?

"Oh, I can't say that. It'll upset her."
I hear this from guys ALL THE TIME.
Maybe she needs some blunt honest truth.
Maybe she needs to know you are a human being with actual feelings.
Maybe you need to tell her what you think, how you feel.

Maybe you need to learn how to talk to her/him.
Maybe she/he needs to learn how to listen to hear you.
Not just listen to respond to you.

So many things in life could be solved with a conversation.
Not an assumption.

#adaywithdori
#haveaconversation
#withoutloudwords
#listentounderstand

Toxic Women.
This is a thing.

It's a thing that happens much too often.
There is so much chatter about how the man is always the bad guy.

That isn't always the case.

Guess what?
Sometimes women are toxic.
They know how to

- manipulate
- turn the tables
- get their way at all costs
- play the victim
- point the finger

The list goes on and on.

As a society we've taught men to

- be tough
- not show emotion
- give and give
- brush it all off

This list goes on and on.

It's a well-known fact that I have a long list of guy friends, and I joke about being the Ann Landers of the construction world.

The things some of these guys have been through emotionally because of toxic women would blow some people's minds.

It's not okay.
It's not something they talk openly about very often.
It's not something society accepts.

My opinion on this matter is really very simple:
The man in your life is your partner.
He is not your personal bank account.
He is not someone you can repeatedly belittle and demean.
He is not someone you order around.
He is not someone that is there to fix all your problems.
He is there to be supportive and an equal.

If the way you speak to him is the way you would be comfortable being spoken to,
No problem.

If it's not,
Take a long hard look in the mirror.

Remember this:
Your children are watching.
Would you be comfortable with your son being treated or talked to the way you treat his father
Or
Do you want your daughter to treat her future spouse the way you treat yours?

#adaywithdori
#dontbetoxic
#menhavefeelingstoo
#bearollmodel
#dontdestroyagoodguy
#counselingisagoodthing

Brace yourselves. I have something to say that will blow your mind.

Girls and guys can be friends. And nothing more than just friends. It is true! I promise.

Since I was single forever. The number one question I got asked when I was in a relationship was, "Is this guy okay with you driving a truck" Now if you truly know me, the answer is obvious. Why would I date someone that has an issue with my career? Of course, he was fine with it.

Here's the deal people. Everyone makes friends somewhere along the way in life. Some are going to be male/female friendships. It's okay! You do not give up your friends for a relationship.

What you do is be open and honest about your friends. Every time I talk to a guy about more than work stuff, I let my S/O know we talked that day. I'm probably not going into full detail because being the "Ann Landers" of the trucking world means confidentiality.

However, I don't lock my phone. He knows where I'm at, who I'm with, and where I sleep at night.

When you've been single for a while and then have someone special in your life, you are supposed to want that person to know ALL your friends—Girl or guy, it isn't supposed to matter. You want your friends to be happy for you.

If you have "friends" that no longer contact you or respond because "OMG, you're in a relationship." Newsflash! They were not your friend in the beginning. You had something they wanted, which obviously they can no longer have.

You are allowed to have friends. You are allowed to have a past.

You are not allowed to purposely make someone jealous. That's childish and rude.

#adaywithdori
#friendsareimportant
#neverbetoldyoucanthaveafriend
#openhonestupfront

I've recently seen a number of posts from women wishing their husbands helped them more.

Some of these women are absolutely at their wit's end from exhaustion—mental and physical.
Add on top of that a non-supportive spouse.
She's going to lose her s— on you.
Here's the deal, guys:

Her place as your wife is to be your partner, not your parent.

You live there to

- help out
- do the dishes
- cook meals
- do laundry
- help with the kids
- know the schedules
- take care of getting the kids' places

Do not
Wait for her to

1. ask you
2. tell you
3. lose her s— on you

Be her partner.
Stop thinking it's her "job."

Most of all,
Listen to her and truly hear what she is saying,
Then make the appropriate adjustments in your relationship.

I promise you there is a difference between venting to you at the end of the day and asking you to help her out.

If she has gotten to the point that she says these words,
"I need _____ from you."

Nine times out of ten, she has tried and thought of every imaginable way possible to not have to ASK you for help.

Expecting her to ASK you to do something that obviously just needs done is disheartening to a woman.

She sees the dishes need done,
Laundry needs folded,
Garbage needs taken out.
Why do you not see these things?

Stop being selfish.
Be helpful and supportive.

If you're expecting her to do it all,
One day she may just show you she can do it all without you.
It's a partnership, pull your weight.

Women, if you're expecting him to do everything, and you're doing nothing,
Just stop that too.

With school starting or not starting, as the mom, she's concerned about every decision that needs to be made,
So as the husband, don't create more stress in an already stressful time.

#adaywithdori
#justbeherpartner
#bethankfulforher
#treatherkindly

I listened to a great friend yesterday about a recent break up, and it got me thinking.

As you're finding your new normal,
You may possibly find yourself second guessing some choices
Or maybe thinking, "If only I'd done _____ different."

You can "what if" yourself all day long.
It will not fix the problems.

Although it takes two to argue,

It also takes two to communicate.
Remember, some people just don't want to.
You cannot change that.

Maybe you see an amazing side to them and want to encourage them to see it too.
That's great!

Do not ever allow yourself to be belittled, disrespected, taken for granted, etc.
While you're trying to prove to them, they are a good person.

They'll be who they want to be.
Your role in a relationship is to be an equal partner.

So if someone in your life has chosen to become toxic,
Distance yourself.
Do not play into their drama game.
Thank them for the lesson of life and relationships.
Be grateful you learned how not to treat someone.

Grieve for a relationship you never wanted to end.
Take all the time you need.

Do not rush into another relationship to "forget" this one. That simply isn't fair to a future partner.

Just remember: No, you won't die from a broken heart.

#adaywithdori
#distancefromtoxic
#taketimetogrieve
#youdeserverespect

They always say communication is key,
Whether it's

1. work
2. kids
3. coaches
4. other parent
5. relationship
6. coworkers
7. family members

You have to communicate. I wholeheartedly agree.

The bigger part of this equation is listening to understand, not just listening to respond.

What good is communication if what you communicate falls on deaf ears?

Once communication has been established, the hardest part follows: compromise.

So many people still ask me about my relationship with Dean.
Honestly, it was simple.
We listened to each other.
We did not always agree.
We did always respect the others opinions.
We did always do what was best for our kids and our businesses.
That didn't mean we did what was best for him or myself.
It is called being an adult.

#adaywithdori
#listentounderstand
#findacompromise
#mostlybeanadult

The measure of friendship isn't the amount of friends you have.

It's the quality.

It's making a phone call in the middle of the afternoon to your best guy friend saying, "I need your advice, and am I being too girly about this?"
And having him take the ten minutes out his day that you needed.

It's sending a text to your BFF that simply says,
"I'm not okay."
With a response of,
"I know, I'm here."

Everyone in this world has "stuff."

- Some more than others.
- Some less.
- Some deal with it all without blinking an eye.
- Some need that BFF to verbally vomit to on hard days.
- Some hold it all in.

Friendship isn't about fixing each other.
It's simply about being the person you would need if the situation was reversed.

Most importantly, it's about sticking around when life gets messy.

#adaywithdori
#bewhoyouneed
#realfriendsdontdisappear

To all my friends that are basically afraid to be alone,
Your worth in life is not obtained by your relationship status.
Your worth comes from within you.
Work on you. If and when you should be in a relationship, it will happen.

#adaywithdori
#bestthingigottoday
#findyoufirst
#dontbeneedy

A DAY WITH DORI

Today's phone call from my trucker friend:

"Dori, I have two subjects to talk to you about"

Number 1: marriage advice
Not my best subject (obviously) we blundered through.
Poor guy.

Number 2: kids
Mainly older teenage/adult kids
He spoke of his frustrations as a divorced parent.
We discussed ways to approach things differently and having adult conversations with his kids.
He truly just wants to spend time with his kids without it being forced.

What I took away most from this conversation was his regrets from when his kids were growing up,
Which I feel most parents have.

Time management
We get so involved working, cleaning, cooking, getting them into every activity
That we forget to just spend time with them.

I don't mean time going to "the next thing" or helping with homework.
Time just teaching them life.

So as you're raising your little ones, please remember.

They aren't going to remember if the house was spotless every day.
They're going to remember if you took the time to play a game with them.

It truly doesn't matter if they were the BEST in every activity.
It matters if they learned something to help them through life.

There's no need to put them in every sport or activity.
There's no need to compare them to anyone else's child.
There's no need to live vicariously through them.

There is a need to teach them:
Manners
Responsibility
Loyalty
Respect
Hard work
Values
Integrity
Being humble at all times

Teach them the importance of the following:
A few good friends
Being a good neighbor
It's better to show people what you're made of than tell them
And to never forget where you came from

Parenting is hard regardless of your child's age.
Teach them all the way through life.
It'll serve them better in the end.

#adaywithdori
#randomthoughts

I see this kind of posts quite often.
The "I don't have friends anymore."
"My friends are just too busy for me."
"Now that I have kids, no one wants to hang out."

Priorities change
People grow
College
Career
Kids
Relationships

Adulting is hard enough. Don't guilt trip your friends. Maybe be supportive that they have "stuff" going on.
Maybe "hang out" differently then you used to.
As you get older, your circle of friends shifts.
Embrace that.
Make new friends that are at the same stage in life you are.
You don't have to stop being friends with people just because your schedules conflict. Just learn a new way to grow your friendship.
I see one of my best friends a few times a year, and we live about twelve miles apart.
We are busy.
We both understand and accept that of each other.
It's being an adult and wanting the best for each other

#adaywithdori
#dontguilttrippeople
#itsadulting

I've seen these little sayings going around Facebook for a while.

"Who should be served first your husband or your kids?"

If you know me very well at all,
You can probably guess my answer.
None of them, unless they are very young and simply can't make their own plate.

If you are the "man of the house" and make the money
While perhaps your wife is a stay-at-home mom, works part time, full time, or whatever works for your family,
Please do not ever believe you "deserve" for her to serve you your supper.

Remember these:
You are teaching your son how to treat a lady.
You are teaching your daughter how to be treated.
So always treat your wife accordingly.

#adaywithdori
#neverexpect
#alwaysappreciate
#showthemrespectandmanners

Never fight for a place in someone's life.
They will naturally put you where they'd like you to be.
Respect their circle and your placement with in it.
More importantly, respect yourself.
Be careful to not continually

- give more than what's given back
- beg for attention that clearly isn't there
- be an afterthought
- be someone that's only there to curb boredom or loneliness

Not everyone wants the same thing.
That's okay.
It's simply just life.

If it doesn't come simply and naturally,
Let it go

You'll never have to fight for a spot in the right people's lives
Nor will you have to ever wonder if you belong.

#adaywithdori
#neverbegforattention
#itshouldcomenatural
#dontfightfortruelovetruefriends

Every person I talked to today seemed to bring up a communication
conflict somewhere in their life.
Lack of communication leads to a lack of knowing someone else's
feelings,
Which often times leads to assumptions from all involved parties.
We all know that assume simply means:
Ass=u=me
Say what you mean.
Mean what you say.

Listen to comprehend, not just to respond
If you want someone to know how you feel about a situation
Talk to them in your out-loud words while having an adult
Conversation.
Pay attention to not only what's being said,
But also how it's being said.
Tone of voice, mannerisms, facial expressions,
It is all important.
You can truly never resolve an issue with only one party communicating.
Miscommunication or no communication is just a death sentence to
a lot of good things

#adaywithdori
#communicationiskey
#useyouroutloudwords

(Picture of child, both parents and both stepparents)
In my opinion, this should be every parent's goal if they are separated from their child's other parent.

- It's not about liking or disliking each other.
- It's about putting your child first.
- It's about not being selfish.
- It's about being an adult.
- It's about teaching your child about healthy relationships.
- It's about so much more than your hatred for someone your child loves.

If you can't be a grown up and put aside your adult issues for the sake of your child,
At least be quiet in front of them.

#adaywithdori
#justgetalong
#lifestoshort
#dowhatsbestforyourchild

Do not let anyone walk through your life with their dirty feet.

How you allow others to treat you will become reality.
It will become how your children allow others to treat them.
Some people will only be kind and respectful if they are expected to be.

It is okay to not allow yourself to be walked on or disrespected.
It is okay to walk away from someone you may feel is very important
to you but are toxic to your well-being.
It is not selfish to stand up for being treated the way you deserve.
It is okay to take care of you.

#adaywithdori
#wipeyourfeet
#showthemhowtotreatyou

I find myself helping my guy friends out with "girl" advice often. I'm unsure if I'm the correct candidate for their questions, but I do my best to help them.

Here are some recent topics:

- She's mad I don't text/talk to her enough.
  a. Hello, man child, did you text her non-stop to "win her over?" Now you don't feel you need to because you got her? News flash: she thinks you're bored or cheating.
  b. Does he get busy at work and can't text? Be reasonable. He has a job.
- My biggest pet peeve: She wants me to change. What. The. Heck! Girls, why are you dating him if changing him is your goal? Just stop right now. He'll change if he wants to or resent you for forcing him to.
- Girls, stop comparing your lifestyle and/or relationship to others on Facebook. Anyone can have a fairytale life on social media. If you are upset because your friend's husband took her out to dinner four times last week and yours didn't, ask yourself this: Why is she posting that on Facebook? And why do you care? Live YOUR life, with YOUR family. If YOU are unhappy with YOUR life, make changes. But don't make changes because you want to "fit in." You aren't in junior high school any longer.

#adaywithdori

To all my guy friends that say to me,
"Some women are too independent."
"There's nothing I have she needs."

I always say,
"Thank goodness she doesn't need you.
She simply wants you in her life"

Read this:
It's a little long, and you may roll your eyes a time or two,
But this is the gist of it.
If you can satisfy her with a paycheck,
What's saying she'll always be satisfied?
What's saying if you lose your job, she'll stick around?

Make sure she's satisfied with YOU as a human being,
Not your monetary donation towards material things.

#adaywithdori
#wantednotneeded
#thisisagreatread

(This part is not my work. It was a shared on Facebook)

Subject: SELF-WORTH (Very Deep!)

In a brief conversation, a man asked a woman he was pursuing the question: "What kind of man are you looking for?"

She sat quietly for a moment before looking him in the eye and asked, "Do you really want to know?"

Reluctantly, he said, "Yes."

She began to expound. "As a woman in this day and age, I am in a position to ask a man what can you do for me that I can't do for myself. I pay my own bills. I take care of my household without the help of any man or woman for that matter. I am in the position to ask, 'What can you bring to the table?'"

The man looked at her. Clearly he thought that she was referring to money. She quickly corrected his thought and stated, "I am not referring to money. I need something more. I need a man who is striving for excellence in every aspect of life." He sat back in his chair, folded his arms, and asked her to explain.

She said, "I need someone who is striving for excellence mentally because I need conversation and mental stimulation. I don't need a simple-minded man. I need someone who is striving for excellence spiritually because I don't need to be unequally yoked. Believers mixed with unbelievers is a recipe for disaster. I need a man who is striving for excellence financially because I don't need a financial burden. I need someone who is sensitive enough to understand what I go through as a woman but strong enough to keep me grounded. I need someone who has integrity in dealing with relationships. Lies and game-playing are not my idea of a strong man. I need a man who is family-oriented, one who can be the leader, priest, and provider to the lives entrusted to him by God. I need someone whom I can respect. In order to be submissive, I must respect him. I cannot be submissive to a man who isn't taking care of his business. I have no problem being submissive. He just has to be worthy. And by the way, I am not looking for him. He will find me. He will recognize himself in me. He may not be able to explain the connection, but he will always be drawn to me. God made woman to be a help-mate for man. I can't help a man if he can't help himself."

When she finished her spiel, she looked at him. He sat there with a puzzled look on his face. He said, "You are asking a lot."

She replied, "I'm worth a lot."

Send this to every woman who's worth a lot and every man who has the brains to understand!

In my career of choice,
I'm in what most deem a "man's world."
I know this.
I accept this.
I understand this.

I've became great friends with many men over the years.
I'm extremely blessed with these friendships.
I've never been one to take a good person or their friendship for granted.

Mutual respect is something I hold very high in my friendships.

Part of being respectful in my world
does not stop at the person I am friends with.
That respect extends into that person's personal life.
Not every wife, girlfriend, significant other is okay with their guy having friendships with girls.
It is 100 percent okay that they feel this way.
It is not up to me to judge why they feel the way they do. It is my job as the friend to respect how they feel.

So if my guy friends have a partner in their lives that not only accepts me
But chooses to also be a friend to me,
I cherish that feeling.

Adult relationships are hard enough.
There is absolutely no point in making life harder for anyone.

#adaywithdori
#cherishyourfriendships
#respecttheirpersonallife

I just saw an ad to rent a date for Holiday get-togethers.

No one on this earth should feel they have to have a date for a holiday party,
Whether it's a family, friend or coworker gathering.
These are supposed to be the people that
Know you
Love you
Support you
Accept you.

Do not allow them to make you feel less than who you are because you are single.

Instead rock that holiday gathering with the confidence that you don't NEED anyone

As a society, it seems that we are expected to have a relationship status.

How about your status be:
I'm happy with myself
I'm confident in being alone.
I'd rather be alone then in an unhealthy relationship.

Believe me when I say
There are so many worse things in this world than your relationship status being "single."
Love yourself enough to love being alone and confident.

#adaywithdori
#loveyoursinglelife
#takeyourselfonadate

Every man needs a good woman in his life,
Even if she is just a friend.
A good woman adds value to a man's life no matter what capacity
she serves.

To all my guy friends,
You're welcome for being in your life.

But on a serious note,
I think this goes both ways. Good friends add an amazing amount of
value to your life.

Never miss an opportunity to tell your friends thank you. You never
know when it could be the last time you get the opportunity.

#adaywithdori
#friendaaddvalue
#appreciatewhatyougot

I tell my guy friends all the time, "Yes, you should help with the house, laundry, cooking etc. And she should help with the yard, cars, etc. Don't expect to receive if you don't give."

However, the kids, totally 50/50, and guys, you do not "babysit" your children. You parent them.

I love the respect explanation and the part about how you treat your husband at home. Hmmm. What would your friends think of you if they could see you behind closed doors?

If ever you find yourself not being your "regular" self, straying from your beliefs just to please someone else or possibly to avoid a conflict,

Think long and hard before you continue allowing this person space in your life.

Some people will come into your life to encourage you to do and be anyone you want. They will build you up and support you at all that you do.

Then others will come into your life, and they will try to control you, your every move, your circle of friends, the clothes you wear, the hobbies you enjoy, your career of choice, your time with family.

These aren't "good for you people." These are controlling, manipulating, insecure individuals that want you to live the way they say and only their way.

Walk away from this. These people will make walking away difficult. Walk away anyway.

You are made for bigger, better people in your circle. You are made for happiness and joy. You are not to worry about saying hello to someone from your past because it may cause a conflict. You are not to concern yourself with what if "they" aren't okay with your work schedule or outfit today.

This behavior is not a healthy relationship from a significant other, a family member or a really good friend.

It is never okay to allow someone else to call the shots in your life.

#adaywithdori
#neverbecontroled
#justwalkaway

Okay, guys, here's a little advice:

- If she has said no to dinner for three years ago, chances are she truly means no. At this point, you're not wearing her down.
  You're pissing her off.
- If she isn't the only one you randomly ask to dinner, make sure she doesn't know the others or for the love of god,
  Don't talk to her about them.
- If she is busy working, don't tell her she works too much and get all pouty about it. Chances are she is well aware of the hours she puts in and doesn't need to be nagged for trying to better herself.
- Don't invite yourself into her kids' life unless you already know them. Those kids are her whole life, why she works hard, and she isn't going to let you into their lives unless you are beyond amazing.
  Push this, and she'll be done with you.
- Have a hobby. Do not make her your hobby.
  If she's been single and is independent, this is very important.
- Don't walk in thinking you're going to "save" her. First off, if she needs saved, don't bother. Secondly, she isn't looking to be saved, she's looking to be found.
  She wants someone that truly will take the time to know the real her.
- Be genuine. Don't try to impress her with "stuff" or your past. Let her know the real you from the start.
- Just because you don't like being single doesn't mean she has an issue with it.
  Don't ask her if she "plays for the other team" just because you aren't getting what you want.

#datingisdumb
#bereal
#adaywithdori

I listen to the radio. All. Day. Long.

Somedays I even pay attention to the words.

Today as I was listening to this song and scrolling through Facebook, I noticed a lot of my single friends posting about just having broken up with someone or wanting to find a "someone." Posting about cheaters, liars, etc. It came to mind that we should never let someone's lack of interest in us or disrespectful actions weigh so heavy on our self-image. I know we all have, are or will someday, but I'm here to tell you to stop that! Never ever let someone's opinion of you cloud the way you see yourself. It's truly possible they just weren't ready for you in their lives right then. Maybe they have more things in their lives to figure out. Maybe they need time to find themselves. (Yes, this is a thing.) Or maybe they really are a big jerk. Whatever the reason, move on. Do not let them steal your happiness, your life, your thoughts, your self-respect. Sometimes it truly is God's way of saying you deserve so much better. Trust this. Don't dwell on the "could have beens."

Don't let anyone turn your sun ice cold.

#dontletanyonestealyourthounder
#bluelooksgoodonthesky

Blue Ain't Your Color
by Keith Urban

Blue looks good on the sky
Looks good on that neon buzzin' on the wall
But darling, it don't match your eyes
I'm tellin' you
You don't need that guy
It's so black and white
He's stealin' your thunder
Baby, blue ain't your color
I'm not tryna
Be another just
Pick you up
Kinda guy
Tryna drink you up
Tryna take you home
But I just don't understand
How another man
Can take your sun
And turn it ice cold

I saw a post today that made me realize, as a society, we are constantly
blaming others for our heartbreak.

Whether it's a relationship, friendship, family, career, whatever,
We are always quick to say:
"My heart was set on that."
"He/she broke my heart."
"I can't believe he/she would treat me that way. I thought we were
best friends."

The truth is:

- We know when things aren't right.

- We just choose to hang on just maybe something will change.
- We want something to be a certain way so badly we over-look the reality.
- We make excuses.
- We convince ourselves it's alright.
- We are wasting our own time.
- We are breaking our own heart.

You can't make anyone want to be in your life.
Watch their actions.
Then treat them accordingly.
If they don't want you in their life, please don't chase them, thinking they belongs in yours.

#adaywithdori
#stopbreakingyourownheart
#ifyouarentwantedmoveon

Communication is key to any situation.

Take the time to actually say what needs said
In your out-loud words.
Say the hard stuff.

Then don't forget to not only listen to what's being said to you
But take the time to really hear the meaning of what's being said.

No one can read your mind.

#adaywithdori
#communicationiskey
#useyouroutloudwords

This and That

So I guess there's some stupid political deal over University of Wyoming wanting to create a new slogan or whatever with this cute guy as the face behind it all.

"The World Needs More Cowboys."

It's a brilliant slogan for a Wyoming University.

If you truly believe the word *cowboy* means a straight, white, male. You have no understanding of the word.
A cowboy is male or female, young or old, black, brown, white or pink with purple polka dots.
The word defines a tradition,
Not a person.
A tradition lost on some of the next generation.
A cowboy is a friend, neighbor, or stranger.
They are someone willing to lend a hand.
They would give you the shirt off their back. They are the backbone of America (in my opinion).
They take care of livestock and family first and foremost.
They are someone who will stand for what is right, never to be found just following the crowd
They are people of faith
They instill blood, sweat, and tears into a lifestyle few could understand.

This protest or whatever it is about this slogan is a waste of time. These people need to educate themselves on what and who a real cowboy is.

The world does need more cowboys. For they are the ones you will find working to better themselves and their families. Creating a legacy greater then these "protester" people could even begin to imagine.

#adaywithdori
#theworldneedsmorecowboys
#longlivecowboys
#createalegacy

I keep seeing posts that say:
What is wrong with our world?
What is wrong with people?
This generation is horrible.
What has happened to us?
We have happened.
We have a broken system.

The punishment, if there even is one, no longer fits the crime.
Slap after slap on the wrist.

It's all became about rehabilitating everyone.
I am 110 percent in favor of second chances.
However, they have to WANT to change.
They have to PUT in the work.
They have to DO it for themselves.

Not because the courts said,
Not because "it looks good"
But because they want to change.

Instead of focusing so much time on rehabilitating the habitual offenders,
What about focusing on breaking the cycle?
So as a society, we aren't as concerned with the next generation as we seem to be with this one.

This generation is the way it is
Because it is allowed to be this way.

As parents, we have a responsibility to raise good members of society.
If little Johnny is always in trouble, show him actions have consequences.
If you choose not to, please do not complain in twenty years what he has "become."

Instead, look at what you might have created.

Everyone makes mistakes. I've made a pile of them over the years.
Some people learn from them.
Some people will never accept that they need to learn from them.

Be the change you want to see.

#adaywithdori
#societysucks

I watched a little boy throw a temper tantrum in a gas station the other day,
Not a young child melt down, a full-blown tantrum.
His mother was obviously embarrassed as any parent would be.
However, her reaction blew my mind.
She said, "Well, things like this are expected. I'm a single mother."

WHAT?
When did being a single parent become the green light for bad behavior?
Why would you give your child an excuse for poor behavior?
I became a single mom of four kids ages seven, nine, eleven, and thirteen when I was thirty-two.
I didn't plan it. It happened.
We struggled, we fought, we survived, we grew.
At NO time was there ever the excuse they came from a single-parent home.
Don't set your children up for failure with excuses.

#adaywithdori
#iwashardonthem
#notraisingassholes
#zeroexcusesinlife

Let's be serious for a bit.
Life is hard.
Raising kids is hard.
Being in a relationship or marriage is hard.
I talked with an acquaintance this morning that kinda just aired all her dirty laundry to me.
I'm good with that. We all need someone to talk to.

As she was telling me something's going on, I asked her, "Have you said anything?" meaning to her hubby and kids. Her response took me back a bit. "No, I don't want to hurt their feelings. They would be so upset with me."
"Okay, but they are hurting your feelings."
Her comeback was, "Oh, that's okay,"

Which obviously it wasn't or she wouldn't have poured her heart out to me.

Here is my question to you all:
Do people really keep silent and hope things get better? (I see no reality in this course of action.)
Or do they voice their opinion because they are human and have feelings and try to figure things out?
I'm obviously a talk-it-out, fix-it, move-on kinda girl
But first, I am not above telling any of my kids by birth or otherwise they are being an a—hole.

#adaywithdori
#humanfeelings
#voiceyouropinion

I've never once regretted having my kids at an early age.
Now with all the super competitive travel sports, I feel it is an abso-
lute blessing my kids are grown.
I believe there are good and bad in any all things.
I believe a lot of this comes from how the adults in the situation
conduct themselves.
I believe kids should have fun while learning.
I believe they should be allowed the time freedom to be kids and try
out different things.
I believe travel sports is a BIG commitment for everyone involved.
But shouldn't be a full-time job.
I also believe it is a privilege for the child participating.
I believe home, family, and education come first.
I believe, as an adult, if you are representing a team or organization,
you should do so in a professional manner.
If you don't like an answer a parent gives you about their child,
Tough.
They are the parent, and you should respect them
No matter what.

I believe the world needs to go back to the basics.
Not every game played is the World Series.
Let your kids just be kids. Let them play Red Rover, kick ball, tag,
and kick the can.

Every parent wants the absolute best for their kids.
They want to watch their kid succeed and become their best selves.
Please remember this is your child's life to live,
Not your forgotten childhood to force upon your child.

#adaywithdori
#letthembelittle
#dontbeacoachingparent
#letthemfindtheirthing

Say their name.
Tell a story.
Share a memory.

I remember my dad asking me if I thought my sister's friends remembered her.

It's been thirty-three and a half years since we lost her.
I guarantee her friends, to this day, remember so many fun things about her.

I lost my best friend thirty-one years ago this month.
Not a day goes by I don't think of the amazing bond we shared and how much he's missed.

Please don't be afraid to talk about someone that has passed on.

We know they're gone.
We live without them every single day.
We don't have them at holidays or special occasions.
Most importantly, we don't have them in our everyday lives.
We will not ever forget them.
We cherish that you have memories of them too.

In that same thought,
Refrain from the

- I can't believe he's gone.
- You'll never know how much she's missed.
- He was so important to me.

The surviving family is struggling with losing a loved one.
While it's appreciated that you also miss a great person that left too soon,
Please keep the "I can't believe's" to a minimum and just share a special memory.

#adaywithdori
#saytheirname
#gonenotforgotten

As I scroll through Facebook, my heart breaks for the parents trying to do it all right now.

- Family
- Work
- Online schooling
- Referee for your kids
- Your own Sanity

I think back to when my kids were in school.

I do not have a clue how I could have done it all,
Especially being a single parent.

I wish I had some wise words for you all right now.

The best I have is simply

- Not to sweat the small stuff.
- The little ones aren't applying for colleges next year, so give yourself a break.
- The kids are frustrated too. Please don't expect perfection.
- Roll with whatever some days is the best policy.
- Healthy meals are a great idea, making sure they ate today is what's necessary.
- Outdoor PE is a great class no matter how many layers they need to put on.
- You deserve a few minutes to just simply breathe.

Life is a mess for so many right now.

Please try your hardest to not let it get you down.
Don't put added or unnecessary pressure on yourself.
You, your kids, and the teachers are just human.
Everyone is allowed bad moments.
Try not to let them become bad days or weeks.

If you do nothing but complain about online school in front of your kids,
Remember, they may look at that like they've become a big burden for you to balance their schooling with your work.
Watch your words.
It's okay to voice your frustration. Try not to lay blame.

The world is a crazy place.
You have no idea what someone else's life is like. (Even perfect Facebook families have problems.)
So choose to be kind.

#adaywithdori
#taketimeforyou
#nooneexpectsperfection

A DAY WITH DORI

Don't waste the time God has given you.

Too often
"I'll do it later" never happens

Change what you have control of.
Work towards the things you want.

Never miss an opportunity
To call a friend,
Catch up with an old friend,
Make a new friend,

Change jobs,
Start fresh,
Begin a new hobby,
Move out of state.

Take the time today to fix what's broken.

Before
I'll do it later=I ran out of time.

#adaywithdori
#weareonGodstimeclock
#dontbearrogant
#noprocrastination

As the holidays are approaching, I see people posting all sorts of things. Some are excited for festivities; others are dreading them.

Some don't want to go places "single." It's not a plague, it's a relationship status. Being confident enough to not "need" someone in your life is a great accomplishment. Embrace it.

Some refuse to go to certain family gatherings because "we don't talk to them." I truly hope it's a really good reason because someday they may no longer be around to talk to. Hold grudges carefully.

If you have to share your children with your ex and in laws, be thankful! Thankful that their parent wants the opportunity to spend the time with them. Maybe schedules are crazy, maybe it's your holiday, maybe it's inconvenient. More importantly, it's not about you.

Enjoy your holiday. Be kind. Be grateful.

Things I learned in town today:

- Target does not have white-out.
- People that take their dogs into PetSmart should be required to have taken a dog obedience class. Honestly, it's not cute that your seventy-five-pound lab is dragging you around the store.
- Kudos to the mom that explained the value of money to her daughter that wanted an eighty-dollar stuffed unicorn.
- And to the mom whose teenage daughter treated her bad over a pair of jeans you didn't want to buy. This too shall pass.
- The dog locked in the truck in Theisen's was just fine. To the guy that was "going to find his owner," please worry more about child running through the parking lot.

These are reasons I should shop online more often.

#adaywithdori
#imnotjudging
#justtrycommonsense

I've seen over and over posts about poor behavior in kids.

Never fails someone comments.
"This is what happens when we aren't allowed to discipline our own kids."

Who told you aren't allowed to discipline your child?
You aren't allowed to abuse your child.
Huge difference in discipline and abuse.

I raised four kids basically on my own. Dean wasn't much for the hard years of parenting. (It's okay. Please don't blow my phone up. He knew he didn't help much.)

Discipline doesn't mean beating your child.
Discipline is making the wrong thing hard and the right thing easy (much like training a horse or dog. Sorry but true.).

I was never afraid to spank my kids when they were young.
Might have been known to whoop their a—in their teenage years if needed.
I grounded Deaner from working cows with his grandpa at sixteen years old.
I was THAT mom!!

Give them responsibility and respect. You are the parent, not their best friend. Really, honestly don't be your child's best friend.
Also, don't be the warden.
Find a balance, a happy medium. They are going to mess up. It's part of life. Let them figure out how to fix it.
Do not fix it all for them.

Also, do not use the cop out of "I can't do anything about their behavior." You can. It's hard. But you can.

#adaywithdori
#justdisciplinethem
#actionshaveconsequences

Something to remember going into the gift-giving season.
Give a child your time,
Your knowledge,
Your love,
Your talents,
Your humor,
Time can never be bought. Spend it wisely.

#adaywithdori
#givethegiftmoneycantbuy
#yourtime

As I'm sitting in the waiting room at the endocrinologist office today, This poor receptionist has had to explain some information to two different people on the phone. I felt so bad for her I apologized to her for the frustration these patients had caused her.

She was beyond polite, sincere, kind, etc., gave multiple solutions to solve both of their problems. I could hear the one patient yelling at her from across the waiting room through the phone.

What is wrong with people? She is the receptionist. She does not write office policies and procedures. She does not control that another office won't take you. She does not control what your general practitioner will or will not do.

It was clear these patients were not listening to understand. They were just argumentative.

What happened to kindness, understanding, politeness, flat-out acting like an adult?

#adaywithdori
#rudenessgetsyounowhere
#listentounderstand

Don't Be a Jackwagon

We all want our friends to be happy for our happiness, especially if it has been a long time coming.
Then there are the friends.
That just can't be happy for you.

- The ones that always said they would be there for you no matter what until you need them then they back away.
- The ones that suggest you leave that miserable relationship. Then once you do, they want nothing to do with the new person in your life.
- The ones that encourage you to better your career, then are upset that your new career adventure takes up too much of your time.

Some people will just never be happy for your happiness.

These people will break your heart.

However, this gives you the opportunity to acknowledge the happiness of your true friends.

#adaywithdori
#dontbreakhearts
#bearealfriend

Be careful of saying to someone,

"Oh, you'll be fine. You always are."
"You're tough. You can handle it."
"You always land on your feet."

- Possibly it's meant to be a compliment.
- Possibly you think that someone is strong.
- Possibly you believe they'll never falter.
- Possibly you mean you admire their ability to overcome.

What you possibly don't understand and what that person will some-day realize:

- You don't really care how they'll get through it.
- You are going to play your weaknesses against their strengths.
- You're going to worry about you and only you.
- You will always be more concerned with yourself than you ever were for that person.

Having good people in your life should never be taken granted.

Friendships, relationships, family-ships should all be about balance.

When one person is weak, the other is strong.

It is a give-and-take for all parties involved.

Once it becomes one-sided,
When one person is doing all the taking/needing with the mentally of "Oh, you'll be fine,"

A line has been crossed.
You are no longer being respectful of maintaining a healthy relation-ship, friendship, family-ship.

At that point, you are worried about you and only you.

#adaywithdori
#dontbeselfish
#dontbeataker
#strengthshouldntbetakenforgranted

Lying and Dishonesty

Do you feel if you tell your child things like this, it's teaching them to lie?
"Don't tell Dad what we bought."
"We just won't tell Mom I let you do that."

I understand every situation is different. My dad used to tell me when I was younger, "What happens on a trail ride, stays on a trail ride." When we would get home, he would tell Mom everything we did. I always knew he was joking about keeping anything from her.

I'm a black or white type of person, not much area for gray.
My kids grew up in a divorced household. I can't remember a time I was ever okay with the kids lying to their dad or myself encouraging it.

People get upset about "kid's these days."
I wonder if those same people wonder what these kids are being taught, told, and encouraged.

#adaywithdori
#dontlie
#randomthoughts

I'm truly unsure of which is worse.

The liar or the gullible people that believe them.

I'll never understand the point of lying.
I have a hard enough time trying to remember what happens day to day in real life.
Keeping a lie straight would be horrid.

For those that believe the lie,
I'm sorry that you would allow yourself to get pulled into such drama.

Honestly, there is a simple solution.
Don't waste your time caring about the gossip
Or better yet,

Go directly to the source to find out the truth.
Bam, problem solved.

#adaywithdori
#dontbelievealiar
#gotothesource
#stopthedrama

Everyone telling everyone else how to live,

Demanding people to live the way they tell them to.

Just stop.

Not everyone sees life through your eyes.

- rude comments on Facebook posts
- the name-calling

- demanding others to do things your way
- telling others they're selfish if they don't live your way

Why?

First off,
Take a step back and see someone else's point.

- Not everyone has your beliefs.
- Not everyone was raised as you were.
- Not everyone believes everything the media spews out.
- Not everyone chooses to live in fear.
- Not everyone believes masks and social distancing are wrong.

Everyone has their own opinion and reasoning behind it.

Next time you want to "defend" your opinion by posting some link to some article that someone somewhere will say is fake,
Ask yourself if it's worth it
Or
A better idea might be to have an actual conversation about real life
Not a media-driven agenda.

Start with listening to what is actually being said with an open mind.
Don't just hear to respond.
Hear to learn.

Yes, there is a difference

#adaywithdori
#noteveryoneisyou
#heartounderstand
#notjusttorespond

Don't be that person.

Ya know, the one that finds fault in everything someone else does
Yet, still doesn't have their life going in a remotely good direction.

Just think where you could be if you stopped blaming others for
where you are.
Negativity wastes so much energy.

Positive words and actions attract positive people.

#adaywithdori
#dontbenasty

You can only be taken advantage of for so long.
Someday these people that take advantage
of the good someone does for them will ride the karma train for a
good long while.

#adaywithdori
#donttakeadvantage

A DAY WITH DORI

I'll never understand being unnecessarily mean.

Does it make you feel
Important?
Better than others?
Good about yourself?
Inferior?

Couldn't you just roll your eyes and scroll past?
Or just change the subject during a conversation?

#adaywithdori
#sorryaboutcussing
#saynothing

I recently read a post from a stepmom about how she's treated at her kids sporting events by the other parents.

Shame on you if you're a parent that treat the adults in a child's life differently simply because of a title society gave them.

As long as they are good to the child,
Aren't mentally, physically, or verbally abusive,
Then just be kind to them.
You don't have to like them.

It is 100 percent not your business why the child's parents aren't together.
It is 100 percent your responsibility to be a decent human being.

If you chose to treat the "other" adult in a child's life differently, think of the message you're sending to any kids watching your behavior,

Especially your own.
More importantly, theirs.

The world is full of judgmental people.
Don't be one.

The world is also full of blended families.
That doesn't make them less family.
That doesn't make the children less loved.

That adult is choosing to be a positive supporter in the life of their significant other's child or children.

You are simply just a teammate's parent
You have no right to make a situation at a school function uncomfortable for anyone.

Be a good example.

Be a nice person.
Smile or say hello.
Make any and all supportive adults welcome.

Although your child's extracurricular activities may be your only time for socializing with your friends,
Don't lose focus that the sole purpose is to be there to support the kids.

Don't be the mean parent.

#adaywithdori
#includealltheparents
#beagoodexample

If you ever hear someone talk bad about me,

You should look them in the eye and say, "You should tell her."

It is entirely possible if more people did this.
There would be less drama, less disrespect, less disloyalty, less put-
ting someone in the middle There is nothing saying you have to like
everyone.
Just don't be immature about it.
Don't like them and go about your day.

Talk to each other, not about each other.

If you can't be kind, at least be quiet.

#adaywithdori
#donttalkbadaboutpeople
#silnceisbliss

There are many things in life that are just none of your business.

Before you say,
"It's just human nature to be curious,"
Please understand that's just a polite way of justifying being nosey.

Unless you are personally involved with something,
It is 100 percent not your concern.

- How the neighbors afford that new boat.
- Where your coworker went on vacation.
- Why your friend is getting divorced.
- What your extended family is doing.

The subject, reasoning or results do not concern you.

Being nosey and meddling in any situation that you aren't a part of is just inviting drama into your life.

If you're the type of person that is so unhappy or bored in your life you have to insert yourself into someone else's,
Please just go get a hobby.

If you only talk to someone else to "get the gossip" or "spread the gossip,"
Do you even have any real friends?
Does anyone even trust you enough to talk to you?
Or do they just tell you what they want others to know?

Every day when you wake up, God gives you a choice of what type of person you can be that day.

Choose wisely so karma doesn't choose for you.

#adaywithdori
#noneofyourbusiness
#dontbeagossiper
#stopbeingnosey

Society is a sad place.

I've said this for year.

If people believe politics is what divided our country
Or that it simply happened in the last four years,
I honestly feel bad for them.

- poor attitudes
- not taking personal accountability
- lack of manners, morals, and values
- thinking others should do things for them

This list could go on and on.

Bottom line:
The world has become a place where people want to hold everyone
expect themselves to a higher standard.

That just isn't the way the world should work.

- Self-accountability
- Live up to the standard you set.
- Before you have an opinion about a subject, you first
  should have an invested interest in that matter.
- Take care of you and yours long before you worry about
  me and mine.

I truly understand everyone has and deserves to have an opinion.

What needs to be reinforced is that, that opinion:

- is not the only one
- doesn't work for every situation
- might be just ridiculous if you truly had all the facts
- should never involve degrading and name calling

You're not always right.
Your child isn't perfect.
Your spouse is only human.
Your career isn't the only one available.
Your family are just people.

We, the people, need to do better.
We, the people, should be teaching our children better.
We, the people, have allowed ourselves to fail.
Only
We, the people, can make this world a better place.
Start at home.
Start with the person in the mirror.

Before your next rude comment on someone else's Facebook post,
Ask yourself:

- Is this a necessary conversation?
- Will my rudeness change their mind?
- Are they open to looking from a different angle?

If not, move on.

#adaywithdori
#expectitfromyourselffirst
#nooneisalwaysright
#wethepeopleneedtodobetter

Listening to Bob and Tom last week. They were talking about ladies that complained about their engagement rings. Apparently, there is an entire Facebook page on this subject.

Then yesterday while shopping at the trade show, I overheard two girls bashing some guy for the ring he bought his fiancée.

What is wrong with people? Seriously!

Ladies,
You are to want to marry the man, not the ring. If you only want a ring that you can flaunt in front of your friends, it's highly possible you are missing the point of the meaning of the commitment you are promising to be making. The size, purity or cut of the diamond is not the measure of his love for you. Instead, possibly look at his love, loyalty, honesty, integrity, how he treats the elderly, children, and his mama. Money cannot buy a good man or a good marriage.
You should want to spend the rest of forever with him regardless if he offers you a Walmart ring or a Helzberg's ring.

Guys,
Every girl has a style or taste. Have some type of idea of this before purchasing a ring. Remember, she is the one wearing it every day for the rest of forever. Make sure it's at least her kinda style.

#adaywithdori
#dontbeungrateful
#itsnotthemoneyspent
#itstheloveinthepurchase

Jealousy.
I'll never understand it 99 percent of the time.
Being jealous of your friend having other friends is a type of jealousy
I find odd.
I have friends from all areas of my life.
Few of these friends are friends with each other.
Two of my closest girlfriends met each other only one time, and I
wasn't even present.
Do you truly desire for your best friend to not have other friends?
If so,
Maybe ask yourself why.
Are you afraid that you'll no longer be a "needed" friend?
If you're only comfortable in a friendship because you're needed and
not wanted,
is that a real friendship?
Will that friend be there for you when you need them most?
Isn't part of a friendship being happy for your friend's happiness?
Whether that happiness includes a whole other set of friends or
maybe accomplishments you've watched your friend work to achieve.
Jealousy truly seems to be a waste of energy in my opinion.

Before you all jump on the,
"This is why I'm only friends with guys" or
"This is why I don't like having girl friends" bandwagon,

Please don't.

Instead, possibly consider how you treat these friends
Or if possibly you are just with the wrong crowd.

All problems aren't always everyone else's fault.
Oftentimes issues could be solved with self-accountability.

#adaywithdori
#jealousyisawastedenergy
#tohaveafriendbeafriend

There is a difference between
Good, honest, blunt truth and
Downright rudeness.

You can get your point across in a mature manner

Without the
"I don't care what you think" attitude.

Because the truth is
You do care what the other person thinks or how they receive your
message.

If you truly didn't care,
Would you be wasting your time?

If you feel like you're not being heard,

Try a different approach:

    o   better tone of voice
    o   nicer choice of words
    o   kinder body language
    o   an openness to understand

If you want them to understand you

Have a conversation in a way they'll be open to:

- less negative
- not attacking them
- speak on to their comfort level

Try listening to the other person also.
Truly listen to comprehend,
Not just to respond.

I'm not saying being rude sometimes isn't necessary.
However, what the other person will remember is your demeanor of rudeness.
Instead leave them with the blunt honest truth.
It is 100 percent up to them to understand or not.
You are better than rudeness.

#adaywithdori
#notimeinmydayforrudeness
#blunthonestyislifechanging
#bewillingtocomprehend

Everyone has a pet peeve.
Mine is dishonesty.
Lies are a waste of everyone's time and energy.

Big lie, little white lie, omitting parts of a story, hiding something.

The truth always wins in the end.
Save everyone's time and just be honest.
Think of it this way,
What costs you more mental stress
Stepping up with the truth or trying to figure out and remember a lie?

#adaywithdori
#todaysrandomness
#justbehonest
#dontwastemytime

Address them privately.

If there is an issue, deal with it like an adult privately.
Never bad mouth someone publicly or to a third party.
Putting someone in the middle of your drama is childish.
It also shows your lack of class, maturity, confidence, etc.

Basically, never let 'em see ya sweat.

#adaywithdori
#riseabove

Sitting in a very crowded waiting room this afternoon. Everyone is quietly talking about what time their appointments were scheduled for and such.

A lady came in a half hour before her appointment, which is great in my opinion. She sat down beside me. Went through her purse/bag seven times. Opened and closed a zip lock bag a few times. Put lotion on her hands twice. Got up to get a different magazine six times. Licked her finger to loudly turn the pages. (This is gross and spreads germs, don't do this.) Opened her zip lock again to get a mint. Made a phone call. Ignored her ringing phone twice but didn't silence it. Sighed loudly A LOT.

Jebb's appointment was at 3:00 p.m. They took him back at 4:15 p.m. This lady's appointment was at 4:00 p.m., and she went to the desk at 4:16 p.m. to let them know they were late getting her in the room. Hellooo. The waiting room is full, almost standing room only. We are all waiting extra time to see the doctor. It's very annoying, but we're all in the same boat.

I understand she might have anxiety about doctor's appointments. Maybe she had somewhere else to be or many different reasons for her rude behavior. However, seriously, be considerate for others in the waiting room with you. Somedays I wonder why some kids are so rude, lack manners, think they are the only person that matters. Then bam, I sit beside a sixty-ish-year-old person and realize some people are just not taught manners.

No worries, she demanded to be seen and was in and out in no time. I'm still in the waiting room as I type this.

#adaywithdori
#bepatient
#stoptherudeness

Be Kind

This may be unimaginable some days, but if you allow someone's poor behavior to affect how you treat them,
You've succeeded in allowing them to control you.

Don't! Just don't!

Always stay true to yourself.
Treat unkind people kindly
With a smile
It's okay. All it will do is confuse them.

Now, I'm not saying let them walk all over you or that you shouldn't stand up for yourself. I'm saying do so kindly.

#adaywithdori
#bekindtotheunkind

What if everyone was just nice to each other?
Instead of being jealous or upset because someone has more "stuff"
than you or goes on more vacations than you,
What if we all just were happy with what we had?
If we aren't happy where we are in life, we choose to change ourselves
for ourselves.
Smile at a stranger.
Tell a single parent what an amazing job they are doing.
Tell her she is beautiful. You may be the only that does.
Be happy for your friend's and family's success.
Be kind.
Be honest.
Be genuine.
Be unique.
Be thankful.
But most of all, be happy!

#adaywithdori
#bekind
#behappy

Life is simple.
We as a society complicate things.
Simple way of life:

- Work for what you want.
- Spend within your means.
- Treat others the way you want treated.
- Respect others things.
- Be a good person.
- Practice kindness.
- Don't lie, cheat, steal.

Complicated life:

- Want what others have but refuse to put in the effort.
- Use others things with no regard to what it took for them to get them.
- Expect someone to bail you out time and time again.
- Blame everyone else for your poor choices.
- Being toxic to those around you.

Stop wanting for more unless you're willing to take risks and put in effort.

Life truly is what you make it. Mistakes and set backs will always happen.
Nothing in life is perfect or free.
Learn to not repeat the past.

#adaywithdori
#bekind
#wantbetterdobetter

What if we didn't focus solely on the bad thing someone said or did?
Everyone makes mistakes of some kind.

Everyone, at one time or another, says the wrong thing,
Whether a slip of the tongue or in frustration of a situation.

That doesn't mean we need to only focus on the negative.

Maybe instead, remember all the positive things this person brings
with them.

No one should be punished for one bad thing.

Everyone is entitled to a bad day.
They should acknowledge their mistake and move on.
They shouldn't have to be continually reminded of a mistake,
Especially if it is a one-time thing.

Give people the benefit of the doubt at least once.

Never forget all the good someone has done.

#adaywithdori
#dontfocusonamistake
#rememberallthegood

I truly believe in my heart of hearts
The people meant to be "That One" have been there.
They've hit rock bottom.
They've been hurt by people that, by society's standards, aren't supposed to hurt you.
They've forgiven people who have never said they were sorry.
They are "That One" because they know what it feels like to be looked over.
To have someone be mean to you.
They know just how much a little bit of kindness can mean to someone.

#adaywithdori
#bethatone

"Raise."
Meaning YOU raise your child—boy or girl—to be polite, respectful, kind human beings.

Not:
Let them do whatever they want.
Let them follow the crowd.
Blame other kids for your child's actions.
Expect things handed to them.

Show them how to live. Don't just tell them.
Ask yourself, *Are you respectful to others?*
Are you a gentleman or a lady?
Do you call others names or belittle them?
And so much more.

Manners begin at home. They begin at an early age. Lead by example. I have always expected my kids to respect me. I've also strived to be a parent my children could respect. In return, I've always tried my hardest to respect my kids. They are their own individual person. I will always respect that while being supportive and encouraging. Part of that is discipline. I will correct them or whoop them if needed to this day. They are fully aware of this.

You, I, or anyone is no better than anyone else. Teach your child this early on, and life will be easier for them for they will feel equal, not more than or less than anyone else.
Character is not a job title or a name on an office door.
It is simply a way of life.

#adaywithdori
#mannersteachem
#showemhow
#bekindtoeveryone

I understand not jiving with someone,
Being annoyed by their behavior.
Let's face it,
Some people are like nails on a chalkboard.

But hate?
You know what hate does?
It exhausts the person doing the hating.
It doesn't normally affect the hated person in the least.
If someone hates you, let them.
I've been unfriended and blocked on Facebook by a few people.
It doesn't bother me in the least. I actually feel sorry for the people that
can't like me because of what I represent, not for who I actually am.

If you hate someone, you have to have a connection to for the rest
of forever.
Hating is going to exhaust you.
Find a way to just tolerate them or the situation.
Life will be much more peaceful that way.

#adaywithdori
#hateisexhausting
#youdonthavetobebffs

There are many things in life I'll never understand.

I try not to dwell on those things.

They are what they are.

I have no power to change others,
Nor do I have the desire.

Nonetheless, my mind still has questions.

Today's thoughts are

- Why bite the hand that feeds you?
- If you want loyalty, be loyal in return.
- If you cheat, steal, or lie, don't expect anyone to trust you.
- No one is the most important person in any situation.
- Treat others the way you want to be treated.
- Society is messed up. You don't need to contribute.
- Kindness goes a long way.
- Your actions show your integrity.

#adaywithdori
#dontcheatstealorlie
#beakindhuman

I had an operator who I don't know tell me the other day,

"You and your son hauled to the first job I ever worked on.
I was a laborer, backing trucks in and had no idea what I was doing.
You guys were the best trucks all day, and when you realized I wasn't
sure what I was doing,
You explained to me what I needed to do:
How to back you in and dump at the best angle and just gave me
some direction.
I've never forgotten that. It was five years ago on the ORA job."

I'll be honest.
I don't remember.
I had to call Dean. Between the two of us, we started to remember
the job.
We have probably been on a thousand jobs since then.

But that day,

We were kind,
And that guy remembered that.
People will never forget how you made them feel.

It's not if. It's how they remember you
—Rascal Flats

#adaywithdori
#kindnessisimportant
#theyrememberhowyoumadethemfeel

I had to shop today, which I hate doing.
(Yes, I know there's curbside availability.)
However, I rarely keep a schedule nor do I typically buy much, so it's
quicker for me to just go in the store.

Society is ridiculous.
I have no other words for it.
It's doesn't matter where I shop,
There are people with no manners everywhere.

There is zero reason to be rude to anyone at the grocery store.
Just go in, do your shopping, pay, leave.

It. Really. Is. That. Simple.
No reason to tell someone else

- what to buy
- what not to buy

And so many other things I heard.

Stop, people.
Seriously.
You do not know anyone else's story.
So please use manners and morals.

However, to the sixteen-year-old cashier I had today,
You, girl, are going places.
And not just because you said I don't look old enough to have grandkids.

Polite, friendly, helpful, kind.
She was so awesome, it made all the ridiculousness easy to ignore.

#adaywithdori
#bekinditsnothard
#youdontknowanyonesstory
#doyourthingandmovealong

I spent the weekend in Louisville at the Circuit Finals Rodeo. It is held during the North American Livestock show.

I cannot begin to explain to you how refreshing it was to be around kind strangers all weekend, whether it was the hotel, trade show, the barns, the food court, or the rodeo.

Doors were held open.
Hats were removed to eat.
"Ma'am" and "sir" were heard everywhere.

At rodeos,
We pray.
We salute the flag.
We sing the national anthem.
We honor the veterans and all those in the military.

Those that don't agree with the going on in Washington DC right now do not disrespect our country by bashing anyone or anything. If they choose to voice their opinion, it's done in a civil and respectful manner.

The agricultural world is the root of America.
I had a lot of faith in human nature restored in my heart the last few days. Being among thousands of people with the same outlook on life.

Our society has become full of hate, name calling, disrespect, and so much more.
Everyone wants to point fingers and place blame. Everyone wants what others have but don't want to work for it.
Our world is actually a really sad place right now.

I'll continue to surround myself with the agricultural community. They make my heart happy.

#adaywithdori
#toomuchhategoingon
#tryrespect
#respectforyourcountry

Sometimes you can see what someone is going through just by notic-ing unusual Facebook posts.

I noticed this yesterday and sent a quick message of encouragement. I don't know this individual super well, more of a very good acquain-tance becoming a wonderful friend.
She sent a very sweet message back saying I was the only person that took the time to reach out.

I'm not posting this for recognition. I'm sharing because kindness has gotten lost in our society.
We all are quick to post funny memes, voice our political opinions, argue about feed rations, whether or not your dog should live outside or if you should blanket your horse.

How often are we just an encourager? Someone that can say, "I've been where you are. It doesn't last forever."
Your encouraging words
may be the only kindness someone receives today.

#adaywithdori
#beanencourager
#bekind

Something to remember:
Every single day,
Instead of criticizing others for how they do things,
Explain a better way.

Instead of thinking only of getting yourself ahead by walking over others, reach down and lend a hand.

Instead of judging someone, ask their story.

Instead of being arrogant and talk like you're better than others,
Look to see how far others have come. Be proud and supportive.

The world is full of hateful, judgmental people.
Don't be one.

Be the change you want to see.
Live everyday day like September 12.

#adaywithdori
#itcostsnothingtobekind
#thinkbeforeyouspeak

Sometimes in life, you will be treated poorly for no other reason than for what you represent, not for who you actually are.
Do not take this treatment personally. Some people will never be able to accept other's decisions in life. It is not your job to try to change their minds.
Be kind. Be you.
Always treat them in a way they cannot speak poorly about you.

#adaywithdori
#treatotherskind

You should never bring yourself down to anyone else's level. Treating someone how they "deserve" might be tempting. But it is a poor reflection on you. Instead, try remembering you are a good person, and possibly the best thing to do is distance yourself. Being the "bigger" person is tough, but treating people badly when you're a good person is worse.

#adaywithdori
#beasgoodasyouare
#notasbadastheyare
#bebetter

The world needs kindness
Now more than ever.

Be a friend.
All this craziness in the world hasn't stopped anyone's life.

Personal problems are still happening.
Financial burdens are more real than ever.
Loved ones are missed.
Raising children is still hard.
Family members are still sick.
Jobs are lost.
Divorces and break ups still occur.
Anxiety is high.
Depression maybe setting in.
Emotions are raw.

Now is the perfect time to

- reconnect with friends that your busy life kept you away from.
- have an actual conversation with someone.
- reach out to someone that might be having a bad day.
- just be there for someone.

Maybe all they need is for someone to listen.
Maybe you need a new conversation topic.

We all need a mental break from the media.

Life should be simpler than it has become.
Society should be kinder.

#adaywithdori
#beafriend
#haveaconversation
#bekind

Bullying is Just Wrong

It's okay to not be liked by everyone.
It's also okay to not like everyone.
What's not okay is:

- bullying
- name calling
- teasing
- just being down right mean

Make sure you show your children this. Preferably by teaching through your example of how you treat others.

#adaywithdori
#itsokaytonotbeliked

I read an obituary on Facebook this morning of a sixteen-year-old boy that took his own life due to bullying.
I understand bullying will always be a "thing."
However, no child is born a bully.
They are allowed or taught to be one.
Respect and kindness are taught at home.
I have often said this to my kids over the years they are a product of their environment.
I'm not saying everyone should love everyone.
That just isn't going to happen.
Everyone can respect others though.

Your children mimic the things you do and say.
Remember to be a good example and sit with the lonely kid in the cafeteria.

#adaywithdori
#bekind
#friendtheoutsider

Bullies,
Don't be one,
Raise one
Or marry one.
I do not believe bullies are born that way.
It's an allowed behavior.
We all know someone that we've heard everyone say, "Oh, that's just how he is."
No! The truth is that's the way he has been allowed or taught to act,
Whether it started at home bullying their siblings or on the bus going to school.
Pay attention to how your kids treat each other or their friends.
And for the love sweet baby Jesus, don't ever say, 'My kid wouldn't ever do that."
Teach them not to!
I bet if your kid knew you might find out,
You're right he wouldn't.
But how about if you knew?
What would you do if you saw your child bullying?
If you allow your kid at five years old to bully and be mean to his peers,
How will they be ever get by in the real world?
A child never corrected turns into a mean adult bully.
I once was told by a woman in her fifties, "He can't help it. He has an anger problem." No, ma'am, your husband is an overgrown spoiled brat because he has been allowed to be.
Having more money, a higher education or being more successful are never a reason to be mean No one is better than anyone else.

#adaywithdori
#randomthoughts
#windshieldtime

So many things in life I'll never understand.
Tonight I'm trying to wrap my head around adult bullies.
I'm unsure if I should be annoyed with them or feel sorry for them.
Their lack of self-esteem and class is second to none.
The more they don't get their way, the bigger jackwagon they seem
to become.
Seriously, if you are like this,
Take more pride and respect in yourself and family.

#keepitclassy
#bullyingisdumb
#dontbeajackwagon

Ya know all those times you've said to someone,

"Oh, that's just how _____ is."

What would happen if you just didn't tolerate that behavior?
What if you choose to walk away?
No argument, no drama,
Just simply remove yourself from the situation or conversation.

#adaywithdori
#donttoleraterudeness
#simplywalkaway

Truest thing I've seen on social media in a while:
"If you are aware your child is being a bully and you choose to support, enable, and defend those actions, you are part of the problem, not the solution."

Being a parent isn't always fun. There will be days your child will disappoint you, possibly even embarrass you. Teach them acceptable and unacceptable behavior. This world can be a big scary place. If they don't realize their behavior is inappropriate because you as a parent never taught them, you are setting your child up for a hard life. One of many disappoints and hardships.

#adaywithdori
#teachthemright
#keepthemhumble
#nobullying

With all the talk in the news right now, I have wondered a few things. First off, I personally don't watch the news or know any of the details. And since it's just about one more celebrity in the spotlight, I really don't care. So please don't blow up my page about that part.

But. I don't believe anyone—male or a female—is born to know how to harass or bully someone. It's learned or accepted behavior.

Think about how many times you have heard,

"Oh, he's just being a boy." How about you teach that boy some manners or respect?

Or

"She just wants attention because she's a girl."
How about you listen to what is being said?

Bullying, harassment, and control will always and forever be a thing. But your response to it can change it. The way you raise your child and treat other people in their presence will show them right from wrong. I'm a firm believer in making life just a little harder for a bully. And by allowing bad behavior, you're actually accepting it. For every big tough guy/girl out there, there is someone a little stronger and a little wiser. These things happen every day. We, as a society, probably need to come up from our phones more often and not accept the behavior of a few bad apples.
Now don't get me wrong. I'm not saying to raise a bunch of pansies. I'm saying teach them right from wrong, to stand up for themselves, even if they have to stand alone, that someone in a position of "power" can still do the wrong thing. Celebrities are just people too and oftentimes allow the fame and fortune to misguide them. Most importantly, teach them that there will always be consequences to poor actions.

#adaywithdori
#bullysareweak
#standupdorwhatsright

Don't Be Judgy

Don't allow anyone to rob you of your happiness.
Not everyone will like you. It's okay. Be true to yourself.
You won't be enough for some people. It's okay. Those aren't your people.
You will be too much for others. That's okay too. Those aren't your people either.
Not every successful person is a college graduate.
Not every college graduate is successful.
Not all young parents are statistics.
Not all single parents need a handout or your pity.
Not all country boys are hicks or rednecks.
Not all city boys are players.
Not all single moms need to be saved.
Not all independent single women are coldhearted.
Not all children of divorce spend their adult lives "recovering" from their childhood.
Not every child with a normal childhood are fully functioning adults.
The world is full of good people. If you can't find one, be one. Raise one. Inspire one.
Don't be judgy.

#adaywithdori
#randomthoughts
#windshieldtime

Judgy people annoy me.
If you want to have a better life,
Create a better life.
You can judge others and make excuses all day long.
At the end of the day, you've made no progress.
You are still where you were that morning.
Never think someone's life is "easier" than yours.
You have no idea what it took them to get where they are in life.

#adaywithdori
#createyourlife
#dontbejudgy

If it's not your life, don't do that judgy thing.

Ya know like,

Oh, they have such an easy life.
They are the perfect family.
He's got a gravy job.
If someone's parents have money, it doesn't automatically mean the
kids do.

If the "perfect" couple splits up,
You don't get an opinion because you aren't part of the relationship.

If someone makes their kid work for everything or gives their kid
everything,
Either way,
Not your business.

Don't have an opinion about a situation that doesn't involve you.

#adaywithdori
#liveyourownlife

I ran across a post this morning.
It was basically a guy talking down to someone else because of his career choice.

Things like this annoy me for so many reasons.

What someone does for a living isn't your business.

If you believe you're "too good" for a certain job,
Kudos to you.

I'll not judge you for the fact that you believe you're better or that you want different for yourself.

I do wonder, however, if you're the type of person to look down on a certain type of career.

Could you still live a comfortable life without someone choosing that career, that one you look down on?

I truly need the blue-collar workers.
I need them every day to survive the life I've chosen to live.

While doctors, nurses, teachers, lawyers are truly needed also,

Try living in today's world without a

- mechanic
- tire guy
- welder (Maybe not everyone needs a welder, but I do.)
- electrician
- plumber
- heating/AC guy

Etc.
You get the point. This list goes on and on.

We need the skilled trades.
Maybe a trade isn't your career of choice,
That's perfectly fine.

However, that doesn't give you the right to talk down to someone else.

What's important is
Having a career you enjoy,
Paying your bills,
Taking care of your family,
Being a good person and productive member of society.

Not being a judgmental jackwagon is helpful too.

#adaywithdori
#dontjudge
#weneedallcareers

It saddens me how judgmental this world has gotten.
How exhausting it must be to waste so much energy having an opinion about things that do not affect you.
This world needs much more kindness and way less judgement.

#adaywithdori
#stayhumbleandkind

Just a reminder with all the weirdness going on with child abductions:

Not all guys in a store are bad guys.

Also, I'll never understand why so many people say,
"I think I was being followed in Walmart, so I rushed out to my car."

How about you turn around, make eye contact, and say, "Can I help you?"
"Do you need something?"
Make THEM uncomfortable.
Make THEM realize you know you're being followed.
They say abductors don't prey on the confident type.
So be confident, even if you're faking it.

#adaywithdori
#todaysthoughts

As I scroll through Facebook, I often see things that say:

"This creepy guy followed me around the store,"
Or
"I didn't like the way the guy at the gas station looked at me."

Now I'll be the first person to say,
Know your surroundings. Pay attention to those people around you.
Don't put yourself in a bad situation.
If it feels off, always go with your gut.

I'll also be the same person to say,

Make sure that creepy guy following you is truly following you and not just aimlessly walking around the grocery store because it isn't something he does much.

The older gentleman that asks what a four-year-old might like as a present could be a grandfather meeting his grandchild for the first time.

The creepy guy at the gas station might not even know he makes you uncomfortable, maybe he's staring off thinking of work, chores, family, etc.

I have many friends that are single fathers of girls.

I had one call me a few years back completely frustrated.

He had taken his daughter to JC Penny to get some new school clothes. She was starting junior high. He says, "I tried to not be the creepy guy hanging outside the dressing room, but at the same time, I wasn't walking away from my twelve-year-old daughter in a department store."
There were mothers there with their daughters also. The comments they made about him to each other were ridiculous. While he under-

stood the situation, being the guy in his mid-forties hanging out at the dressing rooms. He still shouldn't have had to be made to feel he was doing something wrong by taking his daughter shopping.

This world is full of creepy people, ones that are up to no good.

This world is full of judgmental people, ones that will think everything someone else does is wrong.

Be the person that is just kind. If you can't say something nice, say nothing.

Think before you react while keeping yourself safe.
It may seem like a hard balance, but it is a necessary one.

#adaywithdori
#besafe
#besmart
#dontbejudgy

I am so tired of the judgement.

I'm old enough to know that most often, others are judgmental because they are unhappy within themselves.

I just wish instead of judging others, these individuals would just work on improving their own lives.

Find a new career path.
Get different friends.
Start a hobby.
Exercise to clear your mind.
Learn to be a kinder person.

Maybe take a step back.
Look at life at a different angle.
Put yourself in someone else's position.
Try all of these things before being judgmental.

I promise you aren't perfect.

#adaywithdori
#dontbejudgy
#thinkforyourself

These are the things I heard today:

- Why'd you cut your hair?
- Why don't you buy a newer truck?
- No one understands why you work with Dean.
- Why do you have those bulls around?

I get all kinds of questions about an array of things in my life regularly. I'm fine with all of it. However, other people may not be okay when questioned about their personal life choices. I get how people are curious about things in others' lives. But is it your business why someone does something?

#adaywithdori
#dontbejudgy
#askmyreasons

First let me say,
I love Facebook.
I enjoy staying in touch with family and friends, reconnecting with old friends along with making new friends.
When I don't like something someone posted, I simply scroll past.

Recently, I've noticed my friends explaining and defending their personal life choices on their Facebook pages.

Some have defended their decision of how they have chosen to co-parent with their ex.

Some have defended their decision to be a stay-at-home parent.

Some have defended their decision to take an out-of-town job.

Why in this world is any person made to feel they need to defend their personal life choices to their Facebook FRIENDS?
Aren't your friends supposed to be the ones to support your life choices no matter what?

At times in life, we might have to make decisions that in a perfect world we wouldn't have to make. Just maybe those decisions are made to just survive, get through a crisis, get to the next step. Instead of making your friends feel they need to explain themselves to you on Facebook, how about you be their friend? Because let's be honest,

if they are explaining themselves on Facebook, it's because they've heard rumors, and no one went directly to them, which might be exactly what they need—
A friend to talk to, not an added burden of thinking Facebook is the devil.

No one has a perfect life, there is plenty of hate and disappointment in this world. Be a friend. Unless you are living inside the same walls, do not judge a situation you aren't living.

#adaywithdori
#bekind
#dontbejudgy

"Well, you know how you can be."

I've heard this so many times in my life.

I never really understood this.
And it always bothered me.
I always thought to myself,
No, I guess I don't know how I can be.

One day I was talking to my friend, Chris, about this. Thankfully, he explained it to me.

He said,
"You don't tolerate nonsense.
You intimidate people simply by who you are.
You do your own thing.
You don't ask for anything.
You don't even know you're different and that makes you scary to some people."

I live my life simple.
Be kind.
Be helpful.
Be honest.
Be respectful.
Work hard.
Always hustle.

I treat people how I want to be treated.
If I'm disrespected, I'll question you on that.
Apparently, others don't like that much.

#adaywithdori
#dontbejudgy
#becarefulwhatyoutolerate

None of us are perfect.
Some of us have been through more than others.
We all deal with our dramas differently.

At the end of the day,
No one should be judged

If you can't reach out and say I've been there and I'm here for you,

Please just don't be judgy.

#adaywithdori
#bethereforsomeone
#dontbejudgy

I've said this before, and I will continue to say it.
Do not be judgy.
(Yes, I know that probably isn't a real word.)

You have absolutely no idea what someone else's life is like. You have
no idea how bad of a day someone might have had.

You are not living anyone else's life. Concentrate on living your life.
Leave others to live with their peace or their demons. It is their choice.

#adaywithdori
#dontbejudgy
#bekind

People truly need to stop being judgy, especially when it comes to raising kids.

Every parent is going to do things for their kids differently.
Every family has different hobbies and interests.

I'm not looking for justification on how I raised my kids. I'm simply showing an example of different lifestyles.

I've heard this a million times,
"Your kids are so lucky to have grown up with horses. Must be so nice to be able to afford all that."
In some ways, yes, my kids are extremely lucky, most definitely. When there's chores to do when it's -20 windy and snowing or 95 degrees in the shade, and they are fixing fence. I bet they would argue that. Owning livestock has taught them responsibility, sacrifice, loss, hard work, etc. We have sold more than one good horse. Bought our share of bad ones. We have buried a few great ones. We all have had broken bones or stitches along the way.

They've also done without a lot of things other kids have.

We never went on vacations without it involving a rodeo or horses.
We never went to amusement parks or skiing.
We never attended all the cool concerts or neat shows at the I-Wireless Center.
My kids didn't do travel sports and stay in hotels every weekend.

Please do not judge another family's hobbies or passion. It may seem to you they have "way more money" than you have. If this is your opinion, soon it will be your child's opinion. Then it will turn into bullying or snobby comments. In reality, they probably just chose to spend differently.
We don't have a big fancy house or go out to eat very often. We've never went to Chicago shopping. Heck, we rarely went shopping locally. I couldn't tell you the last concert I went to. Movie theaters

aren't a regular thing either. It's a lifestyle we choose. Just because we live and spend differently does not mean we have more. It simply means we have different priorities.

#adaywithdori
#dontbejudgy
#differentpriorities

Create Your Life

There is a reason it is called the past. Leave it there. Continually reliving it will rob you of the present and more importantly, the future. Cherish the memories. Learn from the mistakes. Then move forward. Your future self will thank you for it, so will the people you surround yourself with.

#adaywithdori
#startthenextchapter

My life is far from what I "planned." I'm sure most of you could say the same thing about some aspect of your day-to-day life. Don't dwell on it. Don't get lost in the "wishing I'd done this or that." Live the life in front of you. Sometimes, for whatever reason, your life takes a different path, one you didn't think you'd ever travel down, more than likely, one you may not have even chosen. Travel the hell out of that path. Enjoy it. Don't live with the what-ifs or I-should-haves.

#createyourfuture
#livelife

People will always throw stones in your path. It depends on you what you make of it—a wall or a bridge. Remember, you are the architect of your life. A successful person is one who can lay a firm foundation with the bricks that others throw at them!

#adaywithdori
#buildyourfirmfoundation

Snapchats like these are just neat.

A little time to reflect
How far our boys have come,
How watching them do what they love is priceless,
How well they can work together,
How there's truly little they can't do,

Life gets busy doing the next thing.

We often forget to enjoy the moment.

Even if that moment is a simple Snapchat that to some is just trucks, trailers, and cornstalk bales,

To me it's
Hard work,
Teamwork,
Achieving goals,
Watching little boy's dreams become grown men reality,

Don't get so busy living life that you forget to enjoy the view along the way.

#adaywithdori
#enjoytheview
#createyourlife
#littleboysdreams
#grownmenreality

I get accused of being boring often. I don't go out much. I have a hard time staying awake past 9:00 p.m. I've been accused of being married to my work. I don't take sick days. Vacations usually involve a bucking stock sale or a trail ride. No, I do not feel I'm "missing out" on life. I'm a simple girl, living a simple life that I've been fortunate enough to create for my family.

I have goals. BIG goals! It takes hard work to achieve goals. If you aren't working hard towards your goals, you, my friend, have dreams!

#adaywithdori
#neverslowyourhustle
#createyourfuture
#goalgetter

I heard someone use these words the other day in a conversation: "Victim Mentality."
A great many of us have been "victims" of some sort of bad situation.

Our response to the situation is what paves the way for our future.

You have a choice:

- to stay bitter and question everything, along with every person in your life for the rest of forever
- or you can choose to grieve for your losses, realize life is not fair, find a way to heal, and move forward

The victim mentality is easier though.
It provides a person with attention.

It gives people an excuse to be a shitty to others.
It allows people to wallow in their own self-pity.

Remember, you can only play the victim so long.
At some point, you'll run out of people to play victim to.

Be your own savior.
Your future self will thank you for it.

#adaywithdori
#dontplaythevictim
#beyourownsavior

Think of this.
Do you want something out of life?
But
You keep talking yourself out if it.
When the next bill is paid off.
When the kids are older.
When you have time.
When you get that raise.

You just can't "justify" doing something for yourself.
Ummm, why not?

You can have results or you can have excuses.
What you can't have is both. Choose wisely.

#adaywithdori
#ditchtheexcuses
#takecareofyou

You are only as limited as you allow yourself to be. Stop the excuses and show some action.

You can do better.

- Lose weight.
- Get a better job.
- Buy a bigger house.
- Get a nicer car.
- Be a better wife, mother, friend.
- You can find more positive friends.

You can. Just do away with the excuses.

#adaywithdori
#ditchtheexcuses

I'm on the go a lot of my life, and as I scroll through Facebook daily, I see all kinds of my friends going out, vacationing, always on the go also.
Then there are nights like last night.
A quiet night mowing.
I love where I live.
Love the life I've created.
Life's too short to be anything but happy!

#adaywithdori
#createyourlife

Not everyone will clap for your success. Unfortunately, I know this first-hand.

But when you get messages like these from an absolute GREAT friend that you haven't talk to in months, it makes you remember, you are on the right track! Surround yourself with the positive!

#picktheflowersholdthestingers
#createyourlife
#adaywithdori

"Being good to yourself isn't corny. It's part of respecting yourself as a worthy human no matter your relationship status or day of the year."

I just ran across the above statement in an article about your relationship status.

I will never understand why people aren't good themselves. We all (especially single parents in my opinion) put our kids' needs and wants way ahead of our way. However, it's okay for you to be good to yourself too. Don't ever wait for someone else to be good to you. Be good to yourself. Take care of yourself. Take yourself out to dinner or to a movie. Make your own plans, you know the ones YOU want to do, not the necessary parent plans or what your husband/wife/sister/ mother etc. wants you to do.
Buy the shoes. (My mom taught me that.)
Take the trip.
Change careers.
Go on that trail ride (my personal favorite).

We all live our lives for our family to provide them a better life. But once in a while, don't forget to do something for yourself so you are a happy person while taking care of everyone else.

Don't ever let your relationship status define you. Being single or in a relationship doesn't make you any more or less of a good person.

#adaywithdori
#takecareofyou
#createyourlife

You are never out of options. You can always rebuild your life. It may not be easy, but it will be worth it.

#adaywithdori
#createyourlife
#buildyourfuture

Is your life in a rut? Change it up. You are not a tree rooted into place. Change can be scary. Scary can be exciting. Exciting life is living. Don't get so busy being safe and secure that you forget to live your life to the fullest.

#adaywithdori
#createyourfuture
#createyourlife

My Trucking World

Let me explain. If you are in the left lane on an interstate, this is the "hammer lane." In this lane, you drive faster than the right lane. If you are not going faster than the car in the right lane, do not use the left lane. If your cruise is set at the same speed as the car you've attempted to pass for the last two miles, adjust your cruise or please just shut it off. You do not, for any reason, ever hangout and drive in the left lane. This lane is reserved for those of us that understand how to drive at a consistent speed, pass, merge, and yield. Seriously, there should be a better driving test.

#adaywithdori
#randomthoughts
#windshieldtime

I believe traveling salesmen should have to go through the same regulations as a big truck driver. I can't begin to tell you how many I see on their tablets, phones, laptops. or my favorite going over paperwork while driving down the interstate.

Do they have hours of service?

Special license because they drive so many more miles than the average commuter?

Random drug testing?

Just because they aren't hauling 80,000 lbs. doesn't mean they aren't dangerous.

#adaywithdori
#randomthoughts
#windshieldtime

Today's driving lesson:
Do NOT pass any vehicle or piece of equipment in a construction zone.
If they have stopped traffic, it is for a reason.

It is not to make you late for work.
It is not to just annoy you.
It is 100 percent because they are doing their job.

Today's example, I was stopped on the road to allow a truck to pull out so I could get into his spot.
Car behind me passed me as the dump truck was turning into the same lane.
Luckily, I was watching in my mirror and was able to stop the truck driver. Although it would have been a mild accident because of low speeds, it would have been a big inconvenience for everyone involved.

We are not out here to
upset you,
make you late
or all the other things you might think.

We are out here doing our jobs.
Please do not make it harder for us.
And for the love of sweet baby Jesus himself, learn the traffic laws and better yet,
Use some common sense.

Lane closure + traffic cones + road work in progress = NO PASSING

#adaywithdori
#commonsense
#constructionzone
#weallwanttogohomesafe

Walking through the trade show. I'm betting I could pick out the drivers that don't use blinkers, understand a four-way stop sign, and can't merge onto the interstate. Life just isn't this challenging.

#adaywithdori
#commonsense
#useyourmanners

I just watched four, count them four cars, go across railroad tracks that had red lights flashing, but no stop arm. They did not do a slow-and-go thing or stop-and-look. They were totally oblivious to their surroundings. Yes, there was a train coming.

Seriously, people, pay attention.

#adaywithdori
#besafe
#commonsense

I'm not a fan of putting the weather forecast on Facebook because seriously, just look outside. However, today it is foggy.

Turn. On. Your. Headlights.

Do. Not. Walk or Bike. Along. The. Roadside.

#adaywithdori
#besafe
#commonsense

Unnecessary things while driving:

- tailgating
- bright lights without dimming
- passing to turn in a block
- staying in the left lane on the interstate
- not knowing how to negotiate a four-way stop sign
- not using blinkers
- not knowing how to merge
- braking on a four-lane for no reason
- not knowing how to go through a roundabout. It's basically four yield signs.
- passing in town when the vehicle your passing is going the speed limit.

#adaywithdori
#ishouldteachdriving
#everyonewouldfail
#commonsense

So glad no one rides in my truck with me. I realized today I talk to myself in utter disbelief of the stupidity of people. They cannot merge into traffic, exit an interstate without slowing down to 45 miles per hour, use turn signals or understand the left lane is for passing.

#adaywithdori
#drivingschool
#commonsense

My old spare truck came in handy last week while my regular ride was in the shop. I hear people ask me ALL THE TIME, "Why don't you buy a new truck?"

It's simple. I don't want to.

Could I? Yes, I could. But I see no reason for it. I'm not much for materialistic status. I'm all about function. My trucks get the job done.

I don't need "approval" from anyone in the trucking/construction world about my truck of choice. You aren't a better truck driver with a pretty truck nor a worse one with an old truck. It's just a job. It's just a truck.

If you want to judge me by my choice of equipment, please judge away. Also know, I don't care about your opinion.

#adaywithdori
#ilovemyoldiron
#imkindaokayatdriving
#dontbejudgy

Whoever decided it was a good idea to allow the person with the most seniority do a job, that someone else is more qualified for, should be forced to worked with them all day, every day.

#adaywithdori

So driving truck has been "what I do" for income for eighteen or so years now. Yes, you will see my truck in random places—Walmart, my chiro office, the hair salon. It's a long way home to get my pickup to do these errands. No, I don't have to "check" with my boss to see if it's okay. No, I don't have a husband to "answer" to about where I have his truck. I'm used to this sort of comments. I also totally understand that my career of choice is not the norm. None of this bothers me in the least; however, it makes you look a little stereotypical to make assumptions. That's my name on the door, son. I shall drive my truck where ever I'd like.

#adaywithdori
#ittrulysaysdorimartentrucking
#dontberude

Had a guy call about getting rock delivered.

Go through figuring out which product and quantity is best for his project.

He explains I'd have to back down the alley into the backyard
Then he asks if that's a problem.

Me: Nope, my truck is handy for jobs like that.

Dude: I meant, are you capable of backing the truck down the alley?
Have you been doing this for very long?

Me: All my adult life. Do you mean can I drive my truck?

Dude: Well, ya, I guess that's what I'm asking.

Me: Nope, you should probably find someone else.

This was an actual conversation.

There was a day in my life I'd go to a job like this to prove I could do it.
Nowadays, I just don't waste my time.

—Play it cool. When involved in the rat race,
You are not a rat nor are you in a race.—

#adaywithdori
#icantevenrollmyeyesthatfar
#ihonestlylaughed
#thisismylife

This may be an unpopular opinion post.

I mean no disrespect to my rancher and farmer friends with this nor do I mean to downplay the hell you've endured with the weather.

The weather has wreaked havoc on the construction industry also. The spring rains made most jobsites impossible to work in. If we could work, it meant putting down a large amount of extra material, which obviously costs someone more money.

Deadlines still need to be met, regardless of weather conditions.

In the weeks we couldn't work, it greatly affected many families financially. That financial effect doesn't just go away, the after effects are felt for weeks, months or possibly years for some.

In the weeks we could work, it was long hours and barely seeing our families.

Spring and fall are not the only times you all need to be patient on the roads. We take longer to get going from a stop. Some of us are a little bigger and need extra room. Sometimes we back in off the roads. Sometimes you may have to be flagged around. Drive through construction cones or follow a pilot car.

While I wholeheartedly agree the farmers feed America,

Please remember the construction worker builds America. We all just want to get home to our families at the end of the day safely.

#adaywithdori
#bepatient
#constructionbuildsamerica

Pulling out of a quarry today.
I see no traffic from either direction; however, the quarry is nestled between a couple curves.

Pickup flies up behind me,
Tries passing me in the double yellow lines on a curve with oncoming traffic.

I slow down to let him get in front of me.
He, all but stops beside me. I speed up for him to get in behind me.
Luckily, the oncoming traffic were also paying attention, and no accident occurred.

Listen, I know that no one wants to be stuck behind the big truck.
No one wants to wait those extra few seconds it takes to get to the speed limit or the extra time it takes us to stop.

While you're trying to figure out how to "beat" the big truck,
I'm trying to find a way to not kill you because that is the reality of you having no patience.
I'm over fifty thousand pounds loaded.
A semi is eighty thousand pounds loaded.
Your car, SUV or pickup will stand little chance in an accident with one of us.

#adaywithdori
#commonsense
#imstartingadrivingschool
#slowdownitllsavealife

Live Right

As the new school year is starting, what if instead of worrying about if your kid

1. made "the team"
2. lucked out and got "the good teacher"
3. drives the coolest car
4. wears the best clothes
5. has the newest phone

What if you made sure they spoke kindly to

1. the new kid
2. their "old" friends
3. the nerd
4. the "uncool" kids
5. the substitute teacher

Remember, your children learn from you. Show them how to be kind.

#adaywithdori
#speakkindly

It is your job as a parent to teach your children real life.

1. "Things" cost money.
2. Going places cost money.
3. Respect is earned.
4. Actions have consequences (both good and bad).
5. Appreciation goes a long way.
6. Manners are required and expected (not an option).
7. Chores are necessary.
8. Learn to do things for yourself.
9. The job as their parent isn't to do for them but to teach them to do for themselves.

Without basic life skills, your children are being set up for failure in the real world.

#adaywithdori
#teachthem

A good explanation of the difference between ethics and morals:

"The ethical man knows he shouldn't cheat on his wife,
Whereas the moral man actually wouldn't."

Society lacks morals in many walks of life.

Many people feel like if they "don't get caught,"
Then it's not morally wrong.

At the end of the day,
If you breathe a sigh of relief because you
"got away with something,"

Did you actually do good in life
Or
Did you just not get caught doing a wrong?

I'm a very firm believer in
If you don't want it done to you, don't do it to anyone else.

It will ultimately always be your choice

1. how you live your life
2. how you treat others
3. if you tell the truth
4. if you're deceitful

Make sure those choices are ones that let you sleep at night.

Only you can live up to your own moral standards.

#adaywithdori
#moralstandards
#liveright

Many of you know that encouraging my kids to chase their dreams and teaching them there really is more to life than work is very important to me. "Love what you do, and you'll never work a day."

Newt posted this today. These words make me smile. We, as a society, complicate life in ways that do not need to be complicated.

Just maybe this child of mine does listen to my wisdom.

> The most deathly beautiful thing about life
> is that it has an end. You can't worry about
> the end, though. You don't have to know
> who's going to be there in the end, how you're
> going to get there or even where you're going.
> Just know, as long as you're living for your
> dreams and you're happy, you're living right.
> —Dean Marten

#behappy #beblessed #bethankful

As the holidays approach, please remember this.

You do not owe anyone affection!

Blood does not give anyone a free pass to mistreat you.

You know in your heart if you are a good person or not. Please do not let the opinion of a "family member" interfere with your inner peace.

You should not feel guilty for not loving them at your full capacity. They should rethink their own actions that has pushed you to an arm's length of affection.

#adaywithdori
#yourpeaceisimportant
#youdoyou

I began my Thanksgiving day watching old Western movies with my grandbaby. Thankful for Grit TV when you don't have cable. Had brunch with my whole family at my daughter and son-in-law's. Ended my Thanksgiving festivities at Lady Di's where all of Emery's grandparents (on her momma's side) were all together. As I drove home, I realized how lucky that little girl is. Dean and I may be divorced, but we are still friends. We both get along great with each other's parents. And above all, we are all still a family for our kids and granddaughter. It was not always this way, but God willing, it will stay this way for our future.

#blessedwithfamily
#lifeisgood
#itsabouttheyounguns

Every family has certain traditions.

It is okay to carry them on.

It is also okay to make new traditions.

It's okay to do what's best for your family, your spouse, your kids, yourself.

Don't allow the pressure of "this is when we've always done dinner" stress you out.

Newly married
Newborns
Toddlers
Blended families
Extended families

Things change throughout life.
Don't lose sight of the real meaning.
It's about getting together to celebrate as a family.
The date on the calendar or the time on the clock isn't what's important.
It's who's around the table that truly matters.

#adaywithdori
#stressfreeholidays
#keepitsimple
#dontlikeitdontcome

The kids and I have drawn names the last few years for Christmas. It saves on how much everyone spends and is just simpler. Last year as we opened presents, we talked about how crazy it is that we even get each other presents because we don't need anything. We are the type of family if you need something, go get it. So this year, we will be adopting a family or two and doing more for those who need help. The kids have all agreed this is a great idea. I'm awful proud of them for not being materialistic and realizing that they may not have everything they want, but they do have everything they need.

But of course, Emery will get presents. Christmas is for the little ones.

They may have agreed with this because I hate to shop.

On days I think I've screwed this parenting thing all up, Moments like this remind me it's all good.

#adaywithdori
#rememberthereasonfortheseason
#givemorewantless

I've seen a post floating around saying something along the lines of "Don't brag about having your Christmas shopping done because there are others that haven't started or don't know how they'll afford Christmas this year."

While I truly understand the meaning of the post,
I have to wonder,
Is that fair to ask your friends to not share their

1. joy
2. relief
3. good intentions

I don't know what they may have had to sacrifice to have their shopping finished already.

I don't know nor do I care what they bought.
Maybe everyone in their family is getting socks this year.

Maybe they had to cancel a planned vacation,
So they decided to spend their money elsewhere.

What I do know is this:

I am never going to ask my friends to not share something with me that makes them happy.

I wouldn't be much of a friend if I turned their happiness around to make it about my misfortune.

#adaywithdori
#everyonehasadifferentpath
#youcouldjustbehappyforthem
#itsnotaboutyou

I was asked today
if I'm always so sassy.
"Is there any other way to be?" was my response.

#adaywithdori
#keepitclassy
#sassyandbadassy

Know Your Worth

Be secure with your own self
Talking down about someone says more about your own character
than it will ever say about who you are speaking of.

#adaywithdori
#knowyourworth
#keepitclassy

I don't say this often, but it was a very tough week.
I'm more of a tomorrow's-a-new-day kinda girl.
I roll with the punches fairly easily.
This week was different.

I realized loyalty is something I give easily but don't get much in
return.
I found out no matter how much you help others, some people just
wouldn't appreciate your efforts.
I've always believed in you get what you give.
This week I've learned what you allow is what you get.
Some people just make the mean side of you surface.

It was a gorgeous night.
As I drove up my driveway and noticed my place,
I remembered where I started and how far I've come.

So here's to a new tomorrow.
Remember, people treat you the way you allow yourself to be treated.

#adaywithdori
#sooverthisweek
#iowasunset
#lovemylife

I've been a lot of things.
I've worked my way up from places I never thought I'd get out of.
I had bad days, hard days, impossible days.
But I never ever stopped working hard for what I wanted and needed.

#adaywithdori
#neverslowyourhustle

Never let others get so comfortable with your good heart that they forget you have feelings.

Set boundaries.

Say no.

Don't let them take advantage of your kindness.

Expect appreciation. It's just good manners for others to see what you'll do for them.

#adaywithdori
#dontsetyourselfonfire
#expectthemtobekind
#dontbetakenadvantageof

Start today for a better tomorrow.
If you never step out of your comfort zone,

1. You'll never know how far you can really go.
2. How happy you can really be.
3. How good you could really feel.

No one can do it for you, but plenty of us will do it with you.

#adaywithdori
#stepoutofthecomfortzone

Stop with excuses.
Stop with negativity.

Stop with self-doubt.

Just do because you're badass like that.

#adaywithdori
#bebadass

A conversation and a Facebook post I saw today made me realize
something very important that so many of us do not value ourselves.
We tend to try to make everyone else's life better, easier, more fulfilling.
We put up with being disrespected and pushed aside.
We make up excuses why those we love treat us as an option.
I lived that life once.
Believe me when I say if you see no change, run out of options, just
are plain exhausted from the toxic ways of others,
Walk away for your piece of mind.
You are a person of value.
You cannot make someone else see your worth.
If they don't see it,
Why would you think they deserve you?

#adaywithdori
#youarevaluable
#knowyourworth

Trust is a precious gift you should never give easily for it isn't the person with whom you put your trust in that gets hurt.
It is you who gets hurt because you thought they were worth it.

#adaywithdori
#trustcarefully

I truly can't believe the rudeness of people.

You can be bluntly honest without being rude.

You can speak your peace without being rude.

You can be real without being rude.

Maybe you need to think of your delivery of the things you're saying.

Maybe you need to say it multiple times in your head before you say it or type it.

Maybe you should reconsider how you'd feel if it was said to you.

#adaywithdori
#justdontberude

"Her happiness is not his responsibility."

Amen. You are not responsible for anyone else's happiness. Don't get me wrong. You shouldn't do things intentionally to create unhappiness in someone's life.

However, people need to find their own happy.
Please never allow yourself to be so dependent upon someone else that you do not know how to be happy without them.
No one needs to be so co-dependent, insecure, controlled, etc. that they can't find their own reasons to smile every single day.

#adaywithdori
#behappyonyourown
#selflove
#dontbeselfish

So. Much. Truth
Don't be that person.

Ya know, the one that finds fault in everything someone else does yet still doesn't have their life going in a remotely good direction.

Just think where you could be if you stopped blaming others for where you are.

Negativity wastes so much energy. Positive words and actions attract positive people.

#adaywithdori
#dontbenasty

So there is the language thing. Sorry about that.

But seriously, I'll be the nicest person ever. However, I promise this. You won't take advantage of my kindness without knowing how I feel about it.

#adaywithdori
#iamkind
#donttakeadvantage

It is entirely possible if more people did this,

There would be less drama, less disrespect, less disloyalty, less putting someone in the middle. There is nothing saying you have to like everyone. Just don't be immature about it. Don't like them and go about your day.

Talk to each other, not about each other.

If you can't be kind, at least be quiet.

#adaywithdori
#donttalkbadaboutpeople
#silnceisbliss

Not everyone will appreciate you for who you are or what you have
to offer.
Those aren't your people.
Do not be angry and upset about it.
Simply move on.
Your people are out there.

Always know your worth.

#adaywithdori
#knowyourworth

Once you place a boundary on how you're being treated,
You become the "bad guy."
If your boundaries are that offensive to someone in your life,
Possibly your feelings never mattered much to them.
Never be afraid to love them from a distance.

#adaywithdori
#knowyourworth
#itsaboundry
#neveragrudge

Stop giving the best version of yourself to those who don't appreciate your value.

It will literally emotionally drain you.

Never allow someone that doesn't think you are enough have an opinion.

Remember the importance of seeing the good in yourself even when others are blinded.

#adaywithdori
#knowyourworth
#bevalued

Be secure with your own self. Talking down about someone says more about your own character than it will ever say about who you are speaking of.

#adaywithdori
#knowyourworth
#keepitclassy

Do not ever let someone underestimate you. Be humble, be subtle, be strong, and most of all, be confident. Never let anyone dull your sparkle.

#adaywithdori
#knowyourworth
#alwaysawin

You will be disrespected if you allow yourself to be. It might be hard to leave the table, but believe me in the end, it's better to have pushed through the hard part than to continue to live in a disrespectful world.

#adaywithdori
#knowyourworth
#youdeserverespect

I'm bluntly honest to a fault. However, I was approached the other day by someone that had things to say that had absolutely nothing to do with them or honestly me either. They wanted to make trouble, create drama, and what not. I could have filled them in on so much reality of the situation it would make your head spin. I didn't. What I did, though, was let it bother me. A lot. It really annoyed me that someone could think it's okay to approach someone they barely know and say things that shouldn't be said. That's when I realized I was allowing someone's childish, trashy ways affect me. No one is worth your inner peace. So as my friend Beth would say, "Put those thoughts in a bubble and blow them away."

#adaywithdori
#keepitclassy
#sassy
#andabitbadassy

No one should ever get comfortable disrespecting you. You show people how to treat you by allowing them to treat you in ways far less then you deserve.

If this is you, stop. Know your worth and accept nothing less.

#adaywithdori
#youdeserverespect

What if we just told people what was actually going on in our lives
Instead of protecting the ones that treat their families poorly,
Instead of being embarrassed because of what someone close to us
has done,
Instead of worrying about what society might think,
Instead of being "hopeful" no one will find out.

Just tell it like it is

I've always been a firm believer in
If you don't want someone to know,
Don't do it.

I don't mean only talk badly about other people.
I don't mean constantly complain about a family member.
I don't mean be overly dramatic.
I don't mean expect others to pick a side.

Everywhere you go,
Big town,
Small town,
Work,
School,
Family gatherings,
Kids' sports,
Hobbies,
There will always be rumors.

What if when someone asked you how life was,
You actually told them.

#adaywithdori
#justtellitlikeitis
#whyprotectthosethatdontcare
#justspeakthetruth

About the Author

For nearly twenty-four years, Dori Marten has been an entrepreneur in the dump truck business. During this time, she has inspired hundreds of her Facebook friends by creating *A Day with Dori*. Through these Facebook posts, she describes countless experiences from being a woman in a "man's world" to maintaining a healthy relationship with her ex-husband/best friend while working parallel construction businesses with him and her sons, and raising their four children. When she isn't in the dump truck, one might find her with her granddaughters, horseback riding, videoing bucking bulls, or simply enjoying her backyard view complete with horses, dogs, and an ex-rodeo bull named Sam.

The impact Dori has made on others has not gone unnoticed as many of her Facebook "fans" have continuously asked when she will write a book. For the first time, the woman who is known as a businesswoman, inspiration, rodeo mom, and Nana can now also be known as an author.

CPSIA information can be obtained
at www.ICGtesting.com
Printed in the USA
LVHW110045060922
727645LV00016B/181